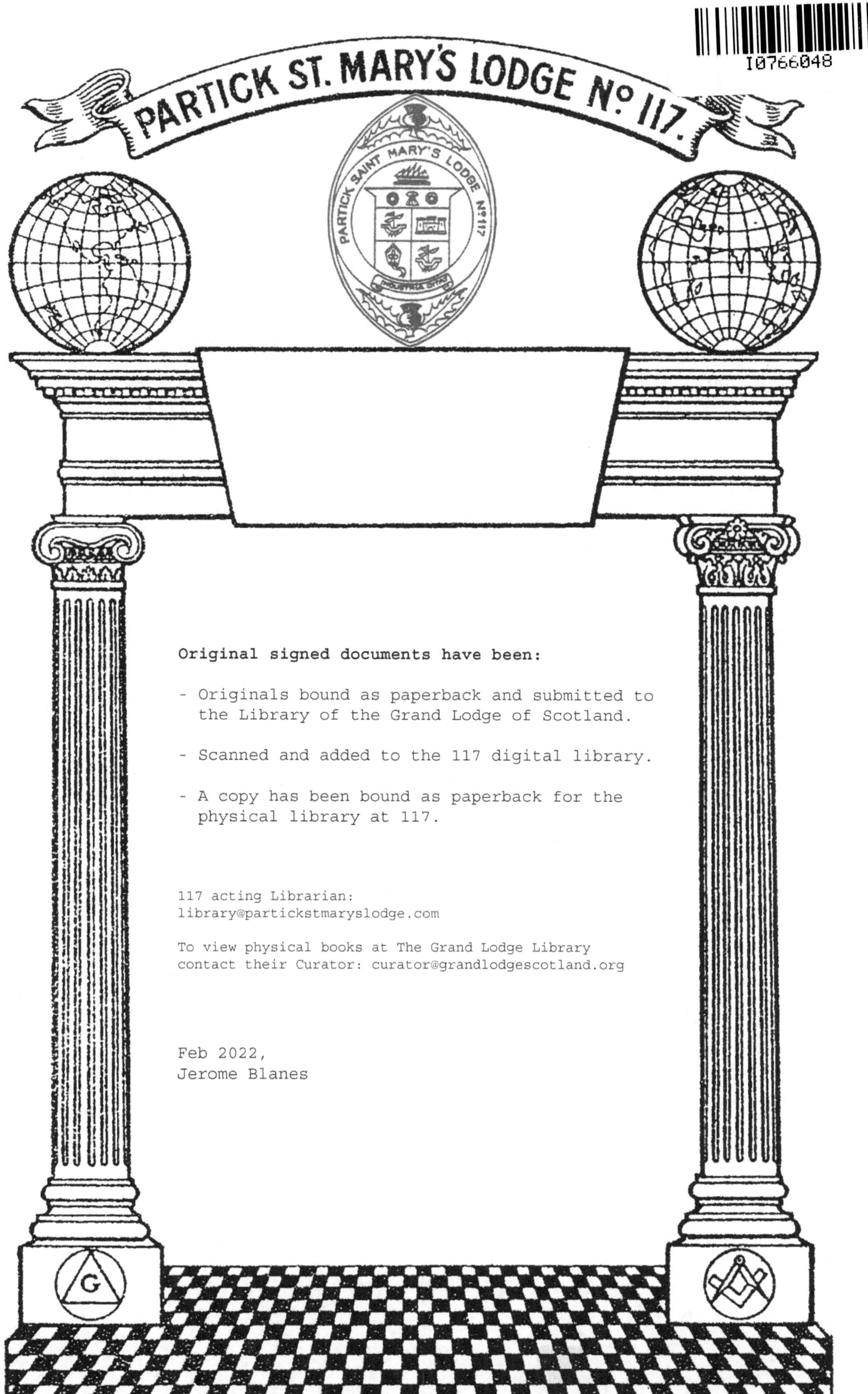

Original signed documents have been:

- Originals bound as paperback and submitted to the Library of the Grand Lodge of Scotland.

- Scanned and added to the 117 digital library.

- A copy has been bound as paperback for the physical library at 117.

117 acting Librarian:
library@partickstmaryslodge.com

To view physical books at The Grand Lodge Library
contact their Curator: curator@grandlodgescotland.org

Feb 2022,
Jerome Blanes

Masonic Temple
92 Dumbarton Road,
Partick
Wednesday 2nd October 2019.

OPENING — A Regular Meeting of Partick Saint Mary's Lodge No 117was held on the above date at 7.15 pm. The Lodge was opened in Due Form and by Prayer in the E.A Degree. The following Brethren were among those present at the opening.

PRESENT

Brother. Alan Cuthill.	Master.
Brother Graeme D. Cameron.	I.PM.
Brother Andrew J. McGroarty.	W.S.W.
Brother James Gallagher.	W.J.W.
Brother Kevin McGowan.	Acting S.D.
Brother David Cumming.	Acing J.D
Brother Petros Karsaliakos	I.G.

A total of 45 Brethren signed the Sederunt Book.

APOLOGIES — Apologies were received from the following Brothers, Robert C. Short P.M. David W. Armstrong P.M.
Brothers Darren Grant, Peter Simpson, Joshua W. Mitchell, Iain Whipp, Scott Small, Mohammad Bachir, Cristian Urlea, Keir Gorman, Donald MacKenzie, Malcolm MacKenzie, Alan M.S. Hopes.
Brothers Fred Christie, Murray Hunter, John Sharp. Hon. Members.

WELCOME — The Master welcomed the Brethren and the visitors into the Lodge, especially Brothers John Gormly P.M. and Kevin McGowan after their recent absence from the Lodge subject to illness. The Master then invited all Reigning and Past Masters to accompany him in the East.

SICK REPOTS — Bro Alex Morrison Almoner stared that Brother Robert C. short P.M. has recently undergone major heart surgery and is now back home and making good progress. Brother Keir Gorman is up in Aberdeen recovering after his recent fall and hopes to be re-joining us soon.

MINUTES — The Minute of the last Regular Meeting held on Wednesday 18th September 2019, having been previuosly circulated was then approved and signed.

CORRESPONDANCE Correspondence was received from the following:
Lodge HLI/RHF No 1459 Annual Installation Friday 25 October at 6.15 pm. Requesting permission to display new Standard within the Temple .
Lodge Salfire No 1505 accepting our invite to confer the M.M.
Lodge Cadder Freestone Installation Saturday 9th November at 3.00pm

ACCOUNTS — Bro Leighton said that there were 2 outstanding Accounts.
G.G. Boilers £134.60 and City of Glasgow Licensing Board £385.00.

APPLICATIONS — There were no Applications Received at the Secretary's Desk.

Secretary   1/   Master

REPORTS — *The Master stated that the monies for the Sponsored Walk should be paid to Treasurer as soon as possible. The Master visited Erskine Home at Anniesland and the Glasgow Lodging House Mission and presented cheques for £300 each on behalf of the Lodge. Brother Douglas Smith stated that while on holiday to California he visited Torrance Masonic Centre and witnessed a third degree The Master thanked all who participated in Glasgow Open Doors, a total 410 persons came through our doors over the 2 Days. We think that P.S.M.L. were the first Masonic body to take part in this event. By all accounts this was a great success not only for Freemasonry in general but for this Lodge in particular. All good feed back from what we hear. The Master thanked all who attended the W.D.L.A., where Brother Ian Barkley was the runner up in the pool competition .*

INTIMATIONS — *Provincial Grand Lodge Dinner Dance on Saturday 6th October within the Glynhill Hotel 5.15pm for 6.00pm*

ALARM — *An Alarm was taken and admitted a large Deputation from Lodge Salfire No 1505, which was headed on this occasion by their Master, Brother John Duncan McGill, The Master welcomed the Deputation into the Lodge.*

RECESS — *The Lodge was adjourned in the Entered Apprentice Degree in order to prepare the Candidate.*

RESUMED — *The Lodge was resumed in the Entered Apprentice Degree. The Master Raised the Lodge to the Third High and Sublime Degree after proving all present to be Master Masons, then presented the Ceremonial Maul to Brother John Duncan McGill, Master of Lodge Salfire No 1505, to enable Lodge Salfire to confer the Master Mason Degree on Brother Ian Barkley. The Office Bearers of Partick Saint Mary's Lodge No117 vacated their Offices in favour of the Office Bearers from Lodge Salfire No 1505.*

ALARM — *An Alarm was taken and admitted the Deacons of Lodge Salfire No 1505 and Petition 18 Brother Ian Barkley, a Fellowcraft of this Lodge. Lodge Salfire No 1505, then Raised Brother Barkley to the Rank of a Master Mason.*

OBLIGATION — *The Obligation on this occasion was conferred by Brother John Duncan McGill, Master, Lodge Salfire Tower No 1505.*

MALLET — *At the conclusion of the Degree the Office Bearers of Partick Saint Mary's Lodge No 117, resumed their Offices and the Lodge was reduced. Brother McGill then returned the Ceremonial Maul to Brother Cuthill with a few well-chosen words of thanks. Brother Cuthill, Master then thanked Lodge Salfire for their rendering of the Master Mason Degree. Brother Cuthill then requested Brother John Monteith, P.M.of Lodge Toryglen Glasgow No 1561, if he would comment on the work of the evening. Brother Monteith first thanked Partick Saint Mary's Lodge. for the welcome extended to all the visiting Brethren when entering the Temple, he then proceeded to compliment Lodge Salfire No 1505 on the quality of the Master Mason Degree.*

Secretary _______________________

Master _______________________

Regular Meeting
Masonic Temple
92 Dumbarton Road Partick
Wednesday 16th October 2019.

OPENING — *A Regular Meeting of Partick Saint Mary's Lodge No 117, was held on the above date at 7.30 pm. The Lodge was opened in Due form and by Prayer in the E.A Degree.*

The following Brethren were among those present at the opening

PRESENT

Brother Alan Cuthill P.M.	*Master.*
Brother. Graeme C. Cameron	*I.P.M*
Brother, Andrew J. McGroarty.	*W.S.W*
Brother James Gallagher	*W.J.W.*
Brother Andrew Buchanan.	*Acting S.D*
Brother Kevin McGowan	*J.D.*
Brother Petros Karsaliakos	*I.G*

and a total of 28 Brethren signed the Sedrunt Book.

WELCOME — *After welcoming the Brethren into the Lodge the Master then invited all Reigning and Past Masters for their assistance in the East .*

APOLOGIES — *Apologies were tendered on behalf of P.M's Brothers' Johm Gormly P.M. Brothers' Darren Grant, Donald MacKenzie, Harry Johnston, Depute Master, Alan Ordish, Jim Ordish, Keir Gorman,*
Hon Members Murray Hunter, Fred Christie, and Alex McLaughlan, Donald Finlayson.

SICK REPORT — *Brother Alex Morrison P.M. Almoner, stated Brother Robert C. Short P.M.was in Rehab, and very cheerful. There was no response to phone calls to Brother Keir Gorman so Brother Almoner presumed that Brother Gorman was still in Aberdeen residing with his Daughter.*

MINUTES — *The Minute of the Regular Meeting held on Wednesday 2nd October 2019, having already have been circulated were then approved and signed.*

CORRESPONDENCE *was received from the following:*
Grand Lodge of Scotland; Moises Gomez Charity Event .
Lodge Union (Glasgow) No 332 Friday 25th October at 6.30pm.
Lodge Riddrie No 1340 Saturday 26th October at 16.30.
Lodge Cadder Freestone No 1584 Saturday 9th November at 3pm.
Lodge Tollcross No 1194 accepting Invite to Confer the E.A. Degree.
CHAS Letter asking for a donation.

ACCOUNTS — *Brother John Leighton Treasurer stated that there were no outstanding Accounts.*

APPLICATIONS *There were no Applications. Received at the Secretary's Desk.*

Secretary   2/4   Master

NEXT MEETING Brother Cuthill stated that our next Regular Meeting will be on
Wednesday 16th October when the Nomination and Election of
Office Bearers for year 2019-2020 will take place.

CLOSED There being no further business the Lodge was Closed in the
Entered Apprentice in Due and Ancient form and by prayer.
The Master wished all a safe journey home and hoped to see
everyone in the not too distant future.

COLLECTION For the General Fund £ 134.60.
For the Jewel and Regalia Fund £54.00.

Secretary

Master.

Prior to the commencement of the Meeting Brother Dale Curless explained
Fire Evacuation Procedures and Safety Procedures should a fire occur.

REPORTS   *Brother Cuthill congratulated Brother MacLeod on receiving*
Honorary Membership of Lodge HLI/RHF No 1459. Brother Cuthill thanked the
Lodge for purchasing his ticket for the Provincial Dance held on Saturday 6th
October and said that every person seemed to enjoy themselves. Sunday 3rd
November , PGL Divine Church Service 2.30pm for 3.00pm

RAISED   *The Lodge was then Raised to the Third or High and Sublime, of a Master Mason*
Degree in due and ancient form after proving all present to be Master Masons. The
Master then declared all Offices vacant, for the purpose of Nomination and Elections
of Office Bearers for Session 2019 -2020.

The Master then brought to the attention of all the Brethren that copies of The
Constitution and Laws of the Grand Lodge of Scotland, opened at Bye- Law 135, The
Bye-laws of the Provincial Grand Lodge of Glasgow, and the Bye-Laws of PartickSaint
Mary's Lodge No 117 being placed in a prominent place
on the dais, opened for inspection.

There being only one nomination for each Office the following Brethren were
Elected into Office for session 2019 – 2020.

Master	*Brother*	*Andrew J. McGroarty*
Immediate Past Master	*Brother*	*Alan Cuthill P.M.*
Depute Master	*Brother*	*By Appointment.*
Substitute Master	*Brother*	*William Duff P.M.*
Senior Warden	*Brother*	*James Gallagher.*
Junior Warden	*Brother*	*Cristian Urlea.*
Secretary	*Brother*	*Graham A. Agnew P.M.*
Treasurer	*Brother*	*John M. Leighton.*
Almoner	*Brother*	*Alexander Morrison P.M.*
Senior Deacon	*Brother*	*Stanley MacLeod P.M.*
Junior Deacon	*Brother*	*Petros Karsaliakos.*
Director of Ceremonies	*Brother*	*Graeme D. Cameron P.M.*
Chaplain	*Brother*	*Kevin McGowan.*
Architect	*Brother*	*Jerome M. Blanes.*
Bible Bearer	*Brother*	*George De Feyter.*
Sword Bearer	*Brother*	*Mohammad Bachir.*
Standard Bearer	*Brother*	*George Ladas.*
Marshal	*Brother*	*Douglas Smith.*
Director of Music	*Brother*	*Donald MacKenzie.*
President of Stewards	*Brother*	*Abbas N. Alhussain.*
Inner Guard	*Brother*	*Andrew Buchanan.*
Acting Tyler	*Brother*	*Cameron A. Gibson.*

Brethren to serve on the General Committee were: The Master, Immediate Past
Master, Senior Warden, Junior Warden, Secretary, Treasurer, Architect, and
Almoner, all Past Master are Ad Hoc

The Brethren to serve on the Enquiry Committee were Master, Immediate Past
Master, Senior Warden, Junior Warden, Secretary, Treasurer, and all past masters
as Ad Hoc.

The Brethren to serve on the Benevolence Committee were: Master, Immediate
Past Master, Senior and Junior Wardens Secretary, Treasurer, Almoner, plus
Brother Stanley MacLeod P.M.

Secretary   2/5   *Master*

The following Brethren were appointed as Auditors Brothers' Keir Gorman and David Morrison PM 88 Hon Mem 117.

REDUCED   The Lodge was reduced to the Entered Apprentice Degree in due form.
Brother Alan Cuthill, Master then asked the Master Elect to say a few words.
Brother Andrew J. McGroarty, Master Elect thanked the Lodge for Electing him into this high Office and also thanked the Office Bearers for allowing themselves to be Elected into their Offices.

NEXT MEETING The Master announced that the next meeting would be a Special Meeting. E.A. Degree conferred by Lodge Tollcross No 1194, on a Gentleman for the outside world.

CLOSED   There being no further business the Lodge was closed in the Entered Apprentice Degree in Due and Ancient form and by Prayer
The Master wished all a safe journey home and he hoped that they may return soon.

COLLECTION   For the General Fund £.95.30
For the Jewel and Regalia Fund £16.50.

Secretary

Master.

Prior to the commencement of the Meeting Brother Alan Cuthill Master explained Fire Evacuation Procedures and Safety Procedures should a fire occur.

Special Meeting
Masonic Temple
92 Dumbarton Road Partick
Wednesday 30th October 2019.

OPENING	A Special Meeting of Partick Saint Mary's Lodge No 117 was held on the above date at 7.30pm. The Lodge was opened in due form and by prayer in the E.A Degree. The following Brethren were among those present at the opening

PRESENT

Brother Alan Cuthill P.M.	MASTER.
Brother Stanley MacLeod.	P.M.
Brother Andrew J. McGroarty.	W.S.W
Brother James Gallagher.	W.J.W.
Brother Douglas Kowal. P.M.	Acting S.D
Brother Harry Johnston.	Acting J.D.
Brother Petros Karsaliakos.	Acting I.G

and a total of 48Brethren signed the Sederunt Book.

WELCOME After welcoming the Brethren and the visitors into the Lodge the Master then invited all Reigning and Past Masters for their assistance in the East .

APOLOGIES Apologies were tendered on behalf of P.M.'s Brother' David W. Armstrong, James S. Hartness,Graeme D. Cameron, John Gormly, Brothers, Dale Curless, Cristian Urlea, Keir Gorman, Kevin McGowan , George Ladas, Andrew Buchanan, Douglas Smith, Rafael Schwarzenergger, Abbas N. Alhussain, Hon. Mem's Brothers' Murray Hunter, Fred Christie, Alex McLaughlan.

PRESENTATION The Master then Presented Brother Donald MacKenzie with his Certificate of Affiliation.

ALARM An Alarm was taken and admitted a large Deputation from Lodge Tollcross Glasgow No 1194, headed on this occasion by their Master Brother Allan McCall. The Master then personally welcomed the Visiting Deputation into the Lodge.
Brother Cuthill then Presented Brother McCall with the Ceremonial Maul enabling Lodge Tollcross Glasgow No 1194 to confer the Entered Apprentice Degree on Mr Alasdair William Agnew.

MAUL The Office Bearers of Partick Saint Mary's Lodge vacated their Offices in favour of the Office Bearers of Lodge Tollcross (Glasgow) No 1194.

ALARM An Alarm was taken and admitted the Deacons of Lodge Tollcross No 1194 along with Petition No 20, Mr Alasdair William Agnew, (son of brother Graham Agnew P.M.), who was then Initated into Freemasonry by The Office Bearers of Lodge Tollcross No 1194.

OBLIGATION The Obligation was delivered by Brother James Cameron I.P.M. of Lodge Tollcross (Glasgow) No 1194.
At the Completion of the Degree Brother McCall returned the Maul to Brother Cuthill, with a few well chosen words of thanks. The office

Secretary   3/   Master

Bearers of Partick Saint Mary's Lodge No 117 then resumed their Offices.

Brother Cuthill thanked Lodge Tollcross (Glasgow) No 1194 for an excellent rendition of the Entered Apprentice Degree.

Brother Cuthill then invited Brother John A. Sharp Master Lodge HLI/ RHF No 1459 to comment the Degree. Brother Sharp firstly thanked Partick Saint Mary's Lodge No 117, for the welcome extended to all the Visitors when entering the Temple. Brother Sharp agreed with Brother Cuthill saying he thought he had just witnessed the best E.A.Degree he had seen.

NEXT MEETING *The Master announced that the next meeting would be a Regular Meeting on Wednesday 6th November 2019 when Partick Saint Mary's Lodge will confer the Mark Ceremonial.*

CLOSED *There being no further business the Lodge was closed in the Entered Apprentice Degree in Due and Ancient form and by Prayer.*
The Master wished all a safe journey home and he hoped that they may return soon.

COLLECTION *A collection was taken for the General Fund which raised £135.80 and for the Jewel and Regalia Fund £56.10*

Prior to the commencement of the Meeting Brother Alex Morrison P.M. explained Fire Evacuation Procedures and Safety Procedures should a fire occur.

Secretary

Master

Regular Meeting
Masonic Temple
92 Dumbarton Road
Partick
Wednesday 6th November 2019.

OPENING   *A Regular Meeting of Partick Saint Mary's Lodge was held on the above date at 7.30 pm. The Lodge was opened in due form and by prayer in the E.A. Degree. The following Brethren were among those present at the opening*

PRESENT

Brother. Alan Cuthill.	Master.
Brother Graeme D. Cameron	I.P.M.
Brother Andrew J. McGroarty	W.S.W.
Brother James Gallagher	W.J.W.
Brother Cristian Urlea	S.D
Brother Kevin McGowan	J.D
Brother Petros Karsaliakos	I.G.

And a total of 40 Brethren signed the Sederunt book.

WELCOME   *Welcoming the Brethren and the visitors into the Lodge, the Master then invited all Reigning and Past Masters for their assistance in the East.*

APOLOGIES   *Apologies were received from the following Brethren:*
Brothers John Gormley, P.M., David W. Armstrong P.M., Robert Angus P.M.
Brothers George Ladas, Joshua W. Mitchell, Darren Grant, Malcolm MacKenzie, Graeme Clarke, Donald MacKenzie, Peter Simpson.
Brothers Murray Hunter, Fred Christie, Cameron A. Gibson, John Sharp Honorary Members.

SICK REPORT *Brother Morrison reported that Brother Robert C. Short P.M. was making excellent progress after his recent Heart Operation. Brother Morrison said that it was nice to see Brother Gorman back in the Lodge.*

MINUTES   *The Minute of the Regular Meeting held on 6th October, which already have been circulated, was approved and then signed.*
The Minute of the Special Meeting held on 30th October, which already have been circulated, was approved and then signed.

CORRESPONDANCE : *Correspondence was received from :*
Lodge Clyde No 408 Installation Friday 6th December last Alarm 19.10.
Lodge Govandale No 437 Installation Sat 2nd November last Alarm 18.20.
Lodge Galen No 1285 Installation Sat 16th November last Alarm 16.45.
Lodge Ballater No 1432 Installation Sat16th November last Alarm 16.20.
Lodge Century No 1492 Installation Mon 11th November last Alarm 18.55.
Lodge Salfire No 1505 Installation Sat 23rd November last Alarm 17.00.
Lodge Cadder Freestone No 1584 Installation Sat 9th November.
Lodge Cadder Freestone No 1584 E.A. Degree Wednesday 8th December.

Secretary   Graham A Ingram.   4/   *Master*

Partick St Mary's Lodge
Regular Meeting
Wednesday 6th November 2019

Lodge Newton Mearns No 1706 M.M.M. Degree 21st November 2019. House of Commons from local MP. Letters of thanks for Bouquets of Flowers Mrs Leighton, Mrs McKirdy

ACCOUNTS *The Treasurer Brother Leighton stated that there were no outstanding accounts.*

APPLICATIONS *No applications were received at the Secretary's desk.*

REPORTS *The Master thanked all who attended the Provincial Grand Lodge Divine Service. He asked for a good turn out for the Service of Remembrance at George Square, meeting in George Street at 10am. The Master stated it was his intention to hold a G.M.C. on Sunday 10th November 2019 at 13.30. Sunday 17th November annual W.D.L.A. visit to Erskine Hospital in afternoon followed by an Instruction Class in the evening.*

RAISED *The Lodge was then Raised to the Third High Sublime Degree of a Master Mason and then Reduced to the Fellowcraft Degree. The Lodge was then recessed. The Degree Team of Past Masters' took up their positions.*

ADVANCED *After proving all present to be Mark Master Masons, Brother Cuthill R.W.M.M. then Advanced the Lodge to the Honourable Degree of Mark Master Mason.*

PETITIONS 13, 14 and 17. *The Lodge being properly constituted and lawfully formed an Alarm was taken and admitted the Conductor along with Petition 13 Brother David M. Cumming, Petition 14 Brother Mohammad Bashir, Petition 17 Ian Barkley, all Master Masons of this Lodge. Brothers Cumming, Bachir and Barkley, were then Advanced to the rank of a Mark Master Mason in a most proficient manner by a team of Past Masters' from Partick Saint Mary's Lodge No 117.*

OBLIGATION *The Obligation on this occasion was conferred by Brother Alan Cuthill Right Worshipful Mark Master of Partick Saint Mary's Lodge.*

REDUCED *At the completion of the evenings work, Brother Cuthill R.W.M.M. closed the Lodge of Mark Master Masons and reopened a Lodge of Fellow Craft. The Office Bearers of Partick Saint Mary's Lodge No 117 resumed their offices. The Lodge was then reduced to the E.A. Degree.*

REDUCED *The Master Brother Cuthill expressed the Lodge's appreciation for the high quality of the evening's labours. The Master then asked Brother Robert McLean Master of Lodge Galen No 1285. to comment on to-nights Ceremonial. Brother McLean, first thanked Partick St Mary's Lodge No 117, for the welcome extended to all the Visitors on entering the Lodge Room this evening and then went to compliment P.S.M.L. on the excellent working of the Mark Ceremonial. The Master said that a special vote of thanks be given to Brother Douglas Kowal P.M. who was Acting Senior Warden during the Mark Ceremonial.*

Alan Cuthill

Secretary   4/10   Master

Partick Saint Mary's Lodge.
Regular Meeting.
Wednesday 20th November 2019.

Regular Meeting
Masonic Temple
92 Dumbarton Road
Partick

Wednesday 20th November 2019

OPENING	A Regular Meeting of Partick Saint Mary's Lodge was held on the above date at 7.30 pm. The Lodge was opened in due form and by prayer in the E.A Degree. The following Brethren were among those present at the opening.
PRESENT	Brother Alan Cuthill. Master.
	Brother Graeme D. Cameron. I.P.M.
	Brother Andrew J. McGroarty. W.SW.
	Brother James Gallagher. W.J.W.
	Brother Cristian Urlea. S.D.
	Brother Kevin McGowan. J.D.
	Brother Petros Karsaliakos. I.G.

And a total of 28 Brethren signed the Sederunt book.

WELCOME	Welcoming the Brethren and the visitors the Master and invited Reigning and Past Masters to accompany him in the East.
SICK REPORT	Brother Morrison informed the Lodge that Brother Harry Johnstone Depute Master was still in Monklands Hospital awaiting results. Brother Robert C. Short P.M. was still making good progress and hopes to attend the Installation. Brother William Duff P.M. had his is Operation and it well.
MINUTES	The Minute of the last Regular Meeting held on Wednesday 6th November 2019, which have already been circulated by E-Mail, was approved and signed.
CORRESPONDENCE	Correspondence was received from the following:

Grand Lodge of Scotland: Re Data Base Forms.
Provincial Grand Lodge of Glasgow: Data Base Data and usage.
Burns Charity Night Marroit Hotel Sat 22nd February 2020.
New Monkland Montrose Lodge: Installation Fri 29/11/19 at 6.30pm.
Invite to confer F.C Degree Mon 11/5/2020.
Lodge St John Whiteinch No 683: Installation Fri 13/12/19 at 6.30pm.
Lodge St Columba No 729 : Installation Fri 29/11/19 at 6.30pm.
Lodge Burns o" Clyde No 1018:Installation Thu 12/12/19 at 6.30pm.
Lodge Eastmuir No 1126: Installation Fri 20/12 19 at 6.30pm.
Lodge Kelvin Partick No 1207: Installation Tue 3/12/19 at 6.45pm.
Invite to confer F.C. Tue 6/10/20.
Lodge Galen No 1285: Invite to confer M.M. Degree Thur 9/4/20.
Lodge Salfire No1505: Invite to confer F.C. Degree on Thur 24/4/20.
Lodge Tower No 1523: Sat 14/12/19 at 3.30pm.

ACCOUNTS	Bro John Leighton Treasurer stated that there were no outstanding Accounts.

Secretary   S/   *Master*

The Master informed the Lodge that our next Meeting would be our A.G.M. followed by our Memorial Service, (Black ties for Senior Office Bearers) which will be conducted by Brother Cuthill Master.

CLOSED   There being no further business the Lodge was Closed in the Entered Apprenticed Degree in due and ancient form and by prayer.

COLLECTION   For the General Fund £95.00.
For the Jewel and Regalia Fund £ 31.50.

Before closing the Lodge the Master invited all present to return for some Lodge Harmony. The Master wished all a safe journey and hoped the see them again in the near future.

SECRETARY   MASTER.

Prior to the commencement of the Meeting Brother Dale Curless explained Fire Evacuation Procedures and Safety Procedures should a Fire occur.

Partick Saint Mary's Lodge.
Regular Meeting.
Wednesday 20ᵗʰ November 2019.

APPLICATIONS Two Applications had been received by the Secretary
1 Mr Saharsh Dave, D.O.B. 16/11/1999. P.O.B. India.
Student at Glasgow University.
Residing at Flat 1014, Scotway House, 165 Castlebank St G11
6EU.
Proposer Bro Mohammad Bachir, Seconder Graeme D.
Cameron.P.M.
2 Mr Sultan Suhail Musa, D.O.B. 4/1/2000, P.O.B Oman, Muscat.
Student at University of Strathclyde.
Residing at Unite Students,1-3 Thurso St Glasgow, G11 6PE.
Proposer Bro Mohammad Bachir, Seconder Stanley MacLeod. P.M.
The Master asked Brother Secretary to write to the Grand Lodge of
Scotland requesting Dispensation for the two Gentlemen, subject to
their age.

INTIMATIONS The Master thanked all who accompanied him to George Square for the
Remembrance Day Service. The Master thanked all the Brethren
who accompanied him to , Erskine Hospital, where the W.D.L.A
presented a Cheque of £1665.00to the Hospital's Manager. The Master
thanked all who attended Lodge St Patrick No 1309, where the
Lodge conferred an Exemplification of the F.C. Degree.

MEMORIAL SERVICE Brother Alan Cuthill Master, then led the Lodge in the Annual
Memorial Service. At the conclusion of the Service the
assembled Brethren acknowledged their appreciation to Brother
Cuthill, Master for another thoughtful Service.

SECRETARY'S Brother Graham Agnew Secretary delivered the Annual Report on
REPORT Lodge statistics for the previous year. This also included a brief report on
the Lodge's 250th Anniversary Celebrations.

TREASURERS Brother John Leighton Treasurer presented his Annual Report,
REPORT comprising of detailed Statement on the Income and Expenditure of the
Lodge's various funds to the year ending 30th September 2019.

ALMONER S Bro Alex Morrison PM Almoner next submitted his Report on behal of
REPORT the Benevolent Fund.

AUDITOR'S Brother David Morrison P.M 88. H.M. 117, and Brother Keir Gorman the
appointed Lodge Auditors, advised that they had examined the books
accounts, vouchers, the Bank Pass Books, and, the Bank Statements and
found them to be presented in a most excellent and proficient manner.
The Balance Sheets dispaying a true and correct view of the Lodge Funds
at that date.

MOTION Brother Graeme D. Cameron I.P.M. Proposed and Brother James
Gallagher W.J.W. Seconded "that the Balance Sheet in it's entirety" be
approved, and there being no one otherwise minded the Motion was
carried.

HONORARIA After some discussion it was agreed that the Honoraria to be paid
remained at the status quo i.e to the Secretary £400.00, to the Treasurer
£400.00 to the Almoner £200.00 and to Tyler £75.00. and Brother

Secretary   5/   Master

13

Partick Saint Mary's Lodge.
Regular Meeting.
Wednesday 20th November 2019.

Stanley MacLeod P.M. be given £100.00

DISBURSMENTS It agreed that this matter of Disbursement to Charities should be left to the general Management Committee of the Lodge.

CLOSING The Master Brother Alan Cuthill thanked the Brethren of the Lodge for granting him the honour and privilege of being Master during our 250th Anniversary year and for the Lodge's loyal support during the year. Brother Andrew J. McGroarty Master Elect on behalf of the Lodge thanked Brother Cuthill, for the service he had given to the Lodge over the past twelve months and for his stewardship of all the Lodge Meetings.

CLOSED There being no further business Brother Cuthill closed the Lodge for the Last time in the Entered Apprentice Degree in due and ancient form and by prayer.

COLLECTION For the General Fund £ 74.50.
For the Jewel and Regalia Fund £ 28.90.

Secretary.   Master.

Prior to the commencement of the Meeting Brother Alan Cuthill, Master informed all present of the Fire Precautions and Evacuation procedures should a Fire occur.

Secretary   5/   Master
                             14

Regular Meeting
Wednesday 4th December 2019
Installation Meeting

Annual Installation
Regular Meeting
Masonic Temple
92 Dumbarton Road
Partick
Wednesday 4th December 2019.

OPENING *A Regular Meeting of Partick Saint Mary's Lodge was held on the above date at 6.45 pm. The Lodge was opened in due form and by prayer in the E.A Degree.*
The following Brethren were present at the opening

Brother Alan Cuthill.	Master.
Brother Stanley MacLeod P.M.	Substitute Master
Bro. Andrew J. McGroarty.	W.S.W .
Bro. James Gallagher.	W.J.W .
Brother Cristian Urlea .	S.D.
Brother Kevin McGowan.	J.D.
Brother Petros Karsaliakos	I.G.

and a total of 92 Brethren signed the Sederunt Book

APOLOGIES Bro John Gormly, P.M. Bro's Robert McKelvie, Joshua W. Mitchell, Abass Alhassan, Grant W. Mitchell Hon Member

WELCOME *The Master welcomed the Brethren and the visitors into the Lodge and thanked them for their attendance and then invited all Reigning Masters to the East and Past Masters to the low East.*

MINUTES *The Minute of the last Regular Meeting Wednesday 20th November 2019, which had previously been circulated were approved and signed.*

CORRESPONDENCE *Correspondence was received from the following:*
Lodge The Gael No 609 Annual Installation Sat 7th Dec at 5.00 pm.
Lodge St Patrick No 1309 accepting invite to confer M.M. Degree on Wed 15th Jan 2020.
Lodge Possilpark No 1330 Annual Installation, Sat 14th Dec at 4.30pm.
Lodge Ruchill No 1436 Annual Installation, Fri 6th Dec at 6.45pm.
Lodge Tower No 1523 Requesting P.S.M.L. to confer E.A. Degree Fri 13 March 2020.

ACCOUNTS *Bro John Leighton Treasurer said that there was 1 Account outstanding*
Ileach Printing Ltd, £0000 for Installation Programmes.
It was agreed pay our just and lawful dues.

APPLICATIONS *Application was received on behalf of .*
Mr Radu Razvan Chirila, 30 Yorkhill Street Glasgow G13 8RY. D.OB.22/6/1997.
Bucherest , Romania , Student at University of Glasgow.
Proposed by Brother Mohammad Bachir, and Seconded by Brother John M . Leighton.
The Master stated that it was his intention to call an Enquiry Meeting followed by G.M.C.

AIMS *The Master asked the Brother Treasurer to read the Aims and Relationships of the Craft,*

ALARM *An alarm admitted a large and distinguished Deputation from the Western District Lodges and Brethren from within and outwith the Province of Glasgow. The Deputation was headed on this occasion by Brother, Alex Ferguson, Master, Lodge Kelvin Partick No 1207. The Master welcomed all the Brethren into the Lodge, and asked for the assistance of Reigning and Past Masters.*

ALARM *A further alarm admitted a Deputation from the Provincial Grand Lodge of Glasgow at the head of the Deputation was Brother Andrew Mushet, Right Worshipful Provincial Grand Master. Brother Cuthill extended the same warm welcome which had been extended to the previous Deputations*

MALLET *The Master Brother Cuthill, tendered the Mallet to Brother Andrew Mushet, pledging the Lodge's fealty to the Grand Lodge of Scotland through The Provincial Grand Lodge of Glasgow. The Right Worshipful Provincial Grand Master thanked Brother Cuthill, for his welcome, and for the token of fealty and thanked the Master for his services to the Lodge over the past year and the returned the Mallet. to Brother Cuthill.*

ALARM *A final alarm admitted the Installing Masters. The Master welcomed Brother Graeme D. Cameron and Brother David W. Armstrong, P.M.'s of Partick Saint Mary's Lodge.*

MALLET *The Master Brother Cuthill, welcomed the Installing Masters into the Lodge and with some regret tendered the Mallet to Brother Cameron R.W.I.M. Brother Cameron thanked him for the Mallet and on behalf of the Brethren of the Lodge expressed to the Master appreciation for his services to the Lodge over the past twelve months.*

Secretary   6/15   Master

Regular Meeting
Wednesday 4th December 2019
Installation Meeting

CEREMONY OF   *The Ceremony of Installation began with the singing of the first two verses of 23 Psalm The Brother Cameron R.W.I.M then asked Brother Secretary to read that portion of the minute of the Election of Office Bearers concerning in particular the election of the Master, was read and after being assured that the Aims and Relationships of the Craft had been read. The R.W.I.M. Brother Graeme D. Cameron requested that the Master present the Master Elect, Brother Andrew J. McGroarty. R.W.I.M, Bro David W. Armstrong, P.M. then read the Ancient Charges and Regulations to the Master Elect..*

OATH DE FIDELI   *Brother, Andrew J. McGroarty Master Elect took the Oath De Fideli which was administered by R.W.I.M Graeme D. Cameron P.M.*

Brother Graeme D. Cameron. R.W.I.M. stated that it was intention to form a Board of Installed Masters to which all Installed Master were cordially invited.

Bro. David W. Armstrong R.W.I.M. then asked the Master Elect to name his Depute. Brother McGroarty stated that he chose Brother Harry Johnstone.

Bro. David W. Armstrong R.W.I.M. then asked Bro Secretary to read the remainder of the Office Bearers Elect.

OBLIGATION   *Brother David W. Armstrong R.W.I.M then Obligated, Invested and Installed the following Office Bearers into their respective Offices:*

Brother Harry Johnston	*Depute Master.*
Brother John McK .Leighton	*Treasurer.*
Brother James Gallagher	*Senior Warden.*
Brother Cristian Urlea	*Junior Warden*
Brother Petros Kalsaliakos	*Junior Deacon .*
Brother Kevin McGowan	*Chaplain*
Brother Jerome Blanes	*Architect.*
Brother George De Feyter	*Bible Bearer*
Brother Donald MacKenzie	*Director of Music.*
Brother Mohammad Bachir.	*Sword Bearer.*
Brother George Ladas.	*Standard Bearer.*
Brother Douglas Smith.	*Marshall*
Brother Andrew Buchanan	*Inner Guard.*

LODGE RAISED   *Bro David W. Armstrong R.W.I.M then Raised to the Third High and Sublime Degree of a Master Mason .*

Brother David W. Armstrong R.W.I.M then adjourned the Lodge and waited on the return of the Installing Board. The Board returned and Brother Cameron R.W.I.M. gave Documentary proof of such, then conducted Brother Andrew J. McGroarty Master firstly to the N.E. corner of the Lodge ,then to the S.E corner of the Lodge, and then Brother Cameron R.W.I.M. conducted the new Master to the S.W. corner and lastly to the centre of the Lodge, before finally, conducting him to the East of the Lodge, where he was placed in the Chair. He was presented with the Charter of the Lodge, Constitution and Laws of the Grand Lodge of Scotland, the Bye-laws of the Provincial Grand Lodge of Glasgow and the Bye-laws of this Lodge, the Volume of the Sacred Law and the Mallet.

PROCLAIMATION   *For the first time and from the East Brother Cameron R.W.I.M. was proclaimed Brother Andrew J. McGroarty,to be Master .and was saluted him as such .*

REDUCED   *The Lodge having being reduced to the Fellow Craft Degree Brother Andrew J. McGroarty, was proclaimed for the second time and from the West that Brother Andrew J. McGroarty,Master and again saluted as such.*

REDUCED   *The Lodge was further reduced to the E.A. Degree, and an alarm taken and two Entered Apprentices were admitted and for a third time Brother Andrew J. McGroarty, was proclaimed as Master and saluted as such.*

CHARGES   *Brother Cameron R.W.I.M then gave the Charge to the Master.*

Bro David W. Armstrong R.W.I.M gave the Charge to the Worshipful Wardens

Brother Curless P.M. then gave the Charge to the Office Bearers, and the Brethren of Partick Saint Mary's Lodge.

Brother Graeme D. Cameron and Brother David W. Armstrong, R.W.I.M. then presented Brother Andrew J. McGroarty with the Mallet and introduced him as Master to the assembled Brethren.

CONCLUDED   *The Ceremony of Installation was concluded by the singing of the first two verses of the 100 Psalm*

Secretary   6/16   Master

Partick Saint Mary's Lodge No 117
Enquiry Committee Meeting
Wednesday 11th December 2019.

Enquiry Committee Meeting,
Masonic Temple ,
92 Dumbarton Road ,
Partick.
Wednesday 11th December 2019.

OPENING   *A Meeting of the above Committee took place on Wednesday Tuesday 11th December 2019, at 19.00.*

PRESENT   *Brother Andrew J. McGroarty.*   *Master.*
Brother James Gallagher   *W.S.W.*
Brother Graham A Agnew P.M.   *Secretary.*
Brother John McK. Leighton   *Treasurer.*
PM's present Brothers Graeme D. Cameron, Stanley MacLeod

APOLOGIES   *Brothers Alan Cuthill, P.M.*

PETITION 21   *An Application for Initiation into Freemasonry having been read on Wednesday 4th December 2019, on behalf of Petition 21 Mr. Radu Razvan Chirila. D.O.B.22/8/1997, Student, Glasgow University, Place of Birth Bucharest, Nationality Romanian. Residing at 30 Yorkhill Street Glasgow G3 8RY.*
Proposed by Brother Cristian Urlea, Seconded by Brother John McK. Leighton, and in keeping with Grand Lodge Law No 168 the Applicant, his Proposer and Seconder, both being in good standing, were this evening interviewed. All having given satisfactory answers to the question asked of them, The Applicant was advised of the procedure which would ensue.

There being no further business the Meeting was Closed with a vote of thanks to the Chair

Secretary   *Master.*

ADDRESS   *The Master Brother Andrew J.McGroarty then gave a short address thanking all the Brethren in attendance and pledging his support to the Lodge for the forthcoming year.*

I.P.M INVESTED   *The Master then invested Brother Alan Cuthill with his Chain of office And then thanked him for the sterling work carried out by himself over the past year. Brother McGroarty, then presented Brother Cuthill, with the IPM Jewel, and Jewel and Bar.*
Brother Cuthill, thanked the Lodge for affording him this great honour.

GRAND LODGE
APPEAL   *The Annual Appeal on behalf of Grand Lodge Benevolence was presented by Brother Alex Morrison P.M.Almoner Elect. The amount collected was £287.00. it was agreed to augment this Collection to the Sum of £300.00.*

PGL RETIRAL   *The Provincial Deputation then retired accompanied by the Installing Masters and invited back for some hospitality.*
Brother Andrew J. McGroarty thanked all for their attendance to-night, and invited all who wished, to return for some Lodge hospitality, and the remainder for a safe journey home ,and haste ye back..

CLOSING.   *The business now having been concluded the Lodge was closed in due and ancient form and by prayer in the E.A. degree*

The Master wished all a safe journey home and he hoped to them back in the Lodge sometime in the not to distant future.

ACTING SECRETARY   MASTER

Prior to the Meeting all present were informed of the Fire and Evacuation Procedures that would be adhered to should a Fire occur.

Partick St Mary's Lodge
Regular Meeting
Wednesday 18th December 2019

Regular Meeting
Masonic Temple
92 Dumbarton Road
Partick
Wednesday 18th December 2019.

OPENING   *A Regular Meeting of Partick Saint Mary's Lodge was held on the above date at 7.30 pm. The Lodge was opened in due form and by prayer in the E.A Degree. The following Brethren were among those present at the opening*

PRESENT

Brother Andrew J. McGroarty.	Master.
Brother Alan Cuthill.	I.P.M.
Brother James Gallagher.	W.S.W.
Brother Cristian Urlea.	W.J.W.
Brother Stanley MacLeod. P.M.	S.D
Brother Petros Karsaliakos.	J.D
Brother Andrew Buchanan.	I.G.

And a total of 29 Brethren signed the Sederunt book.

OBITUARY   *The Master was informed that the new born Grand Daughter of Brother Douglas Smith suddenly Passed away. The Brethren were upstanding as a mark of respect.*

WELCOME   *Welcoming the Brethren and the visitors into the Lodge, the Master then invited all Reigning and Past Masters for their assistance in the East.*

APOLOGIES   *Apologies were received from the following Brethren, Brothers John Gormly, P.M., Robert Angus P.M. Douglas Kowal P.M. Brothers George Ladas, Joshua W. Mitchell, Darren Grant, Malcolm MacKenzie, Donald MacKenzie, Peter Simpson Kevin McGowan, Keir Gorman, Alan Ordish, Jim Ordish, Jerome B Blanes . Brothers Murray Hunter, Fred Christie, John Sharp, Ian Littlejohn Honorary Members.*

SICK REPORT   *Brother Morrison reported that Brother Robert C. Short P.M. was making excellent progress after his recent Heart Operation. Brother Morrison said that Brother Gorman was at Gartnavel Hospital for a Check up. Brother Malcolm Mackenzie was at Gartnavel for Surgery.*

MINUTES   *The Minute of the Regular Meeting held on 4th December, having previously been circulated, was approved and then signed.*

CORRESPONDANCE   *Correspondence was received from :*
Grand Lodge of Scotland : Register of Interests.
         Appointment of an Assistant Grand Secretary.
         Grand Master's Christmas Message.
Provincial Grand Lodge : Masters Diner Friday 31st January 2020.
         Letter of thanks.
Lodge St Vincent Sandyford No553 Lodge Installation Sat 11/1/20 at 3pm.
Lodge Toryglen No 1561 Installation Fri 7/2/20 at 6.40pm.

Secretary   8/19   Master

Partick St Mary's Lodge
Regular Meeting
Wednesday 18th December 2019

*Letters of thanks for Bouquets of Flowers Mrs McGroarty, and Mrs Lewis.
Donation of £20.00 from Brother Robert Angus P.M.*

ACCOUNTS	*The Treasurer Brother Leighton stated that there were no outstanding
accounts. The Treasurer announced that Lodge Diaries were at hand.*

APPLICATIONS	*Two applications were received at the Secretary's desk.:*
1. *Mr Alastair Stewart Martin Reid D.O.B 2 /11/1991. Teacher.
P.O.B. Drumchapel. Nationality British.
Residing at 35 Woodhouse Street Glasgow G13 1AR.
Sponsors Brother Alan Cuthill P.M. Seconder Brother Graeme Clark.*
2. *Mr Roney Cook. D.O.B.27/7/1950. Retired.
P.O.B. Glasgow. Nationality, British.
Residing at 144 Dorchester Avenue Kelvindale, Glasgow G12 0DZ.
Proposer Brother John McKay Leighton, Seconder Brother Stanley
MacLeod P.M.*

REPORTS	*Brother McGroarty thanked all those Brethren who gave him their support
at the following installations, Lodge Knightswood, Lodge Tower,
Dumbarton Kilwinning Lodge .*

INTIMATIONS	*The Master intimated that is was his intention to hold an Enquiry for
the above Gentlemen on Sunday 22nd December at 1400hrs.*

INSTALLATION	*Brother David W. Armstrong R.W.I.M. then Obligated, and Installed the
following Past Masters:*
> *Brother William Duff P.M. as Substitute Master.
> Brother Graham A. Agnew P.M. as Secretary.
> Brother Alex. Morrison P.M. as Almoner.
> Brother Stanley MacLeod P.M. as Senior Deacon.
> Brother Graeme D. Cameron P.M. as Director of Ceremonies*

*Brother Armstrong R.W.I.M stated that only one Officer Bearers to be
Installed.*

LECTURE	*The Master then introduced Brother Robert G. Geddes P.M. 683, H.M.117.
who gave an interesting talk on the various Degrees within the umbrella of
Freemasonry, and was assisted by Brother Cuthill. At the conclusion of the
Lecture both were available to questions. The Master thanked both Past
Masters for the time and effort entailed in the making of a very interesting
and informative talk.*

*The Master informed the Lodge that our next Regular Meeting would be
held on Wednesday 15thr January 2020, which would be a M.M. Degree
conferred by Lodge St Patrick No1309.
The Master extended warm and prosperous Seasonal Greetings to all
present and their respective families.
Brother James Gallagher W.S.W. reciprocated with Seasonal Greetings to
the Master, and his family.
Brother Cuthill thanked the Master for his Stewardship of his first Meeting.*

Secretary Graham A Agnew	8/ 20	*Master* A McGroarty

Enquiry Committee Meeting,
Masonic Temple ,
92 Dumbarton Road ,
Partick.
Sunday 22nd December 2019.

OPENING   *A Meeting of the above Committee took place on Sunday 22nd December 2019, at 14.00.*

PRESENT
Brother Andrew J. McGroarty.	*Master.*
Brother Alan Cuthill	*I.P.M.*
Brother James Gallagher	*W.S.W.*
Brother Graham A. Agnew P.M.	*Secretary.*
Brother John McK. Leighton	*Treasurer.*

PM's present Brothers, Graeme D. Cameron, Stanley MacLeod.

APOLOGIES *Brother Cristian Urlea. W.J.W.*

PETITION 22 *An Application for Initiation into Freemasonry having been read on Wednesday 18th December 2019, on behalf of Petition 22 Mr. Alastair Stewart Martin Reid, D.O.B.2/11/1991, Teacher, Place of Birth Alexandria, Nationality British. Residing at 35 Woodhouse Street, Glasgow G13 1AR. Proposed by Brother Alan Cuthill P.M. Seconded by Brother Graeme Clark, and in keeping with Grand Lodge Law No 168 the Applicant,his Proposer and Seconder, both being in good standing, were this afternoon interviewed. All having given satisfactory answers to the question asked of them, The Applicant was advised of the procedure which would ensue.*

PETITION 23 *An Application for Initiation into Freemasonry having been read on Wednesday 18th December 2019, on behalf of Petition 23 Mr. Roney George Cook, D.O.B.27/7/1950, Retired, Place of Birth Glasgow, Nationality British. Residing at 144 Dorchester Avenue, Kelvindale, Glasgow G12 0DZ. Proposed by Brother John McKay Leighton, Seconded by Brother Stanley MacLeod P.M. and in keeping with Grand Lodge Law No 168 the Applicant, his Proposer and Seconder, both being in good standing, were this afternoon interviewed. All having given satisfactory answers to the question asked of them, The Applicant was advised of the procedure which would ensue.*

There being no further business the Meeting was Closed with a vote of thanks to the Chair.

Secretary   Master

Partick St Mary's Lodge
Regular Meeting
Wednesday 18th December 2019

CLOSED — *There being no further business the Lodge was Closed in the Entered Apprenticed Degree in Due and Ancient form and by prayer.*

COLLECTION — *For the General Fund £68.10.*
For the Jewel and Regalia Fund £ 43.30.

Before closing the Lodge the Master invited all present to return for some Lodge Harmony. The Master wished all a safe journey and hoped the see them again in the near future.

SECRETARY   MASTER.

Prior to the commencement of the Meeting Brother Graeme D. Cameron P.M. explained Fire Evacuation Procedures and Safety Procedures should a Fire occur.

Enquiry Committee Meeting,
Masonic Temple ,
92 Dumbarton Road ,
Partick.
Sunday 22nd December 2019.

OPENING   *A Meeting of the above Committee took place on Sunday 22nd December 2019, at 14.00.*

PRESENT

Brother Andrew J. McGroarty.	*Master.*
Brother Alan Cuthill	*I.P.M.*
Brother James Gallagher	*W.S.W.*
Brother Graham A Agnew P.M.	*Secretary.*
Brother John McK. Leighton	*Treasurer.*

PM's present Brothers, Graeme D. Cameron, Stanley MacLeod.

APOLOGIES *Brother Cristian Urlea. W.J.W.*

PETITION 19 *An Application for Initiation into Freemasonry having been read on Wednesday 4th September 2019, on behalf of Petition 19 Mr. Florion Stefan Niederseer, D.O.B.21/9/1998, Student , Unviversity of Glasgow, Place of Birth Salzburg, Austria, Nationality Austrain. Residing at 20 Cecil Street Glasgow. G12 8RH.*

Proposed by Brother Alan Cuthill P.M. Seconded by Brother Stanley MacLeod PM. and in keeping with Grand Lodge Law No 168 the Applicant, his Proposer and Seconder, both being in good standing, were this afternoon interviewed. All having given satisfactory answers to the question asked of them, The Applicant was advised of the procedure which would ensue.

BALLOT TO BE HELD OVER UNTIL MARCH,(Applicants request)

Secretary   *Master.*

Secretary   **Master**

Partick St Mary's Lodge
Regular Meeting
Wednesday 15th January 2020.

Regular Meeting
Masonic Temple
92 Dumbarton Road
Partick
Wednesday 15th January 2020.

OPENING	*A Regular Meeting of Partick Saint Mary's Lodge was held on the above date at 7.15 pm. The Lodge was opened in due form and by prayer in the E.A Degree. The following Brethren were among those present at the opening*

PRESENT

Brother Andrew J. McGroarty.	Master.
Brother Alan Cuthill	I.P.M.
Brother James Gallagher.	W.S.W.
Brother Cristian Urlea.	W.J.W.
Brother Stanley MacLeod. P.M.	S.D
Brother Petros Karsaliakos.	J.D .
Brother Andrew Buchanan.	I.G.

And a total of 50 Brethren signed the Sederunt book.

OBITUARY — *The Master informed the Brethren of the Passing to the Grand Lodge above of Brother David Thompson P.M. Brother Alex Morrison P.M. Almoner gave a Eulogy on the Masonic career of the late Brother Thompson, whereupon the assembled Brethren were requested to be upstanding for a minutes silence as a mark of respect.*

WELCOME — *Welcoming the Brethren and the visitors into the Lodge, the Master then invited all Reigning and Past Masters for their assistance in the East.*

APOLOGIES — *Apologies were received from the following Brethren, Brothers John Gormly, P.M., Robert Angus P.M. Brothers George Ladas, Joshua W. Mitchell, Darren Grant, Malcolm MacKenzie, Donald MacKenzie, Peter Simpson, Alan Ordish, Jim Ordish, Jerome B Blanes . Brothers Murray Hunter, Fred Christie, John Sharp, Ian Littlejohn Honorary Members.*

MINUTES — *The Minute of Regular Meeting held on Wednesday 18th December 2019 which having been previously circulated by E-Mail, was approved and signed.*

ENQUIRY — *The minute of the Enquiry Meeting held on 11th December was read and the contents therein approved. The minute of the Enquiry Meeting held on 22nd December was read and the contents therein approved.*

BALLOT — *A Ballot was then conducted en bloc on behalf of three Gentlemen,*
1 Mr Alastair Stewart Martin Reid D.O.B 2 /11/1991. Teacher. P.O.B. Drumchapel. Nationality British. Residing at 35 Woodhouse Street Glasgow G13 1AR. Sponsors Brother Alan Cuthill P.M. Seconder Brother Graeme Clark.
2 Mr Roney Cook. D.O.B.27/7/1950. Retired. P.O.D. Glasgow. Nationality, British. Residing at 144 Dorchester Avenue Kelvindale, Glasgow G12 0DZ.

Secretary *Graham A Agnew*   1 of 24   Master *A McGroarty*

Partick St Mary's Lodge
Regular Meeting
Wednesday 15th January 2020.

Proposer Brother John McKay Leighton, Seconder Brother Stanley MacLeod P.M.

3 Mr. Radu Razvan Chirila, D.O.B.22/8/1997, Student, Glasgow University, Place of Birth Bucharest, Nationality Romanian. Residing at 30 Yorkhill Street Glasgow G3 8RY.

Proposed by Brother Cristian Urlea, Seconded by Brother John McK. Leighton.

SICK REPORT *Brother Morrison reported that Brother Robert C. Short P.M. was making excellent progress after his recent Heart Operation and hoped to return to work in the near future. Brother Morrison said that Brother Malcolm Mackenzie was at Gartnaval for Surgery.*

CORRESPONDANCE *Correspondence was received from :*
Provincial Grand Lodge of Glasgow :Quiz Night .
Dumbarton Kilwinning Lodge No 18 invite to confer F.C. Degree on 4/9/20.
St John's Lodge No 46, invite to 275th Anniversary Celebrations 8/2/20.
The Bridgeton and Glasgow Shamrock and Thistle Lodge, accepting our Invitation to confer the M.M. Degree on 1/4/20.
Lodge St Clair Glasgow No 362 Invitation to confer the M.M. Degree on 17/9/20.
Lodge St Skae of Ferryden invite to Brothers Cuthill and Agnew to attend their Festival of St John on 21/2/20.
Lodge Kelvin Partick No 1207 invitation to their Centenary Celebrations on Sat 29/2/ 20 within Partick Burgh Hall.
Lodge Anima No 1223 invite to Installation Saturday 8/2/20 at 4.00pm.
Lodge Galen No 1285 accepting our invitation to confer the M.M. Degree on 19/02/20
Lodge Toryglen No 1561 invite to Installation on Friday 7/2/20 at 6.30pm.

ACCOUNTS *The Treasurer Brother Leighton stated there was one outstanding account. £322. 60 to P.Young for updating Lighting. It was agreed that we paid our just and lawful dues.*
The Treasurer stated that Lodge Diaries were now at hand for purchase.

APPLICATIONS *There were no applications received at the Secretary's desk.*

REPORTS *Brother McGroarty thanked all those Brethren who gave him their support at the following installations, Lodge St Vincent Sandyford and for all the Brethren who attended the festival of St. John at Dumbarton.*

INTIMATIONS *The Master intimated that is was his intention to hold an Office Bearers Meeting followed by a Instruction Class on Sunday 2nd February at 1400hrs.*

ALARM *An Alarm was taken and admitted a large Deputation from Lodge St Patrick No 1309, which was headed on this occasion by their Master Brother Richard W. Beattie. The Master welcomed the Deputation into the Lodge as our "First Foots"*

RECESS *The Master adjourned the Lodge for a short in order to prepare the Candidate. The Master resumed the Lodge.*

MASTER MASON *The Master then presented Brother Beattie with the Ceremonial Maul to enable Lodge St Patrick to confer the McBride Ritual of the Master Mason Degree after Raising the Lodge to the Third and High and Sublime Degree*

Secretary *[signature] Agnew* 18/25   Master *[signature] McGroarty*

of a Master Mason after proving all present to be Master Masons. The Office Bearers of Partick St Mary's Lodge vacated their Offices in favour of the Office Bearers of Lodge St Patrick No 1309.

ALARM — *An Alarm was then taken and admitted Petition No 18, Brother Alan Hopes and the Deacons of Lodge St Patrick. Brother Hopes was then Raised to the Rank of a Master Mason in a most proficient Manner by a team of Office Bearers from Lodge St Patrick No 1309.*

OBLIGATION *The Obligation was delivered by Brother Raymond Black, Past Master of Lodge St Patrick No 1309.*

CONCLUSION *At the conclusion Brother Beattie returned the Maul to Brother McGroarty with a few words of thanks. The Office Bearers of Partick Saint Mary's resumed their Offices, the Lodge was then reduced to the E.A.degree. Brother McGroarty then thanked Lodge St Patrick for an excellent rendition of the Master Mason Degree.*

The Master then invited Brother David Agnew Master of Lodge Thistle and Rose No 73 to comment on to-nights Degree. Brother Agnew first thanked Partick Saint Mary's Lodge for the welcome extended to all on their arrival into the Temple. Brother Agnew then stated that all present had witnessed a very special rendition of the Master Mason Degree.

The Master informed the Lodge that our next Meeting would be a Special Meeting held on Wednesday 29th January 2020, which would be a E.A. Degree on three Gentlemen conferred by Lodge Thistle and Rose No 73.

CLOSED — *There being no further business the Lodge was Closed in the Entered Apprenticed Degree in due and ancient form and by prayer.*

COLLECTION *For the General Fund £127.50.*
For the Jewel and Regalia Fund £ 53.00.

Before closing the Lodge the Master invited all present to return for some Lodge Harmony. The Master wished all a safe journey and hoped the see them again in the near future.

SECRETARY

MASTER.

Prior to the commencement of the Meeting Brother Graeme D. Cameron P.M. explained Fire Evacuation Procedures and Safety Procedures should a Fire occur.

Secretary

Master

Partick Saint Mary's Lodge.
Special Meeting ,
Wednesday 29ᵗʰ January 2020

Special Meeting
Masonic Temple
92 Dumbarton Road Partick
Wednesday 29th January 2020.

OPENING	*A Special Meeting of Partick Saint Mary's Lodge was held on the above date at 7.30pm. The Lodge was opened in due form and by prayer in the E.A Degree. The following Brethren were among those present at the opening*
PRESENT	*Brother Andrew J. McGroarty.* — MASTER.
	Brother Alan Cuthill P.M. — I.P.M.
	Brother James Gallagher. — W.S.W
	Brother Cristian Urlea. — W.J.W.
	Brother Stanley MacLeod . P.M — S.D
	Brother Petros Karsaliakos. — J.D.
	Brother Alan Buchanan. — I.G
	and a total of 46 Brethren signed the Sederunt Book.
WELCOME	*The Master Welcomed Brother Stamatis Theocharous from St George Lodge Cyprus No 3135 E.C. and other visitors, he then welcomed the Brethren and the visitors into the Lodge the Master then invited Reigning and Past Masters for their assistance in the East .*
APOLOGIES	*Apologies were tendered on behalf of P.M.'s Bro's David W. Armstrong, Graeme D. Cameron, John Gormly, Douglas Kowal, Alex Morrison, Brothers, Dale Curless, Harry Johnstone Douglas Smith, Rafael Schwarzenergger, Abass N. Alhussain, Jim Craig, Ian McKirdie, Malcolm MacKenzie. Donald MacKenzie.*
	Hon. Mem's Bro's Murray Hunter, Fred Christie, Alex McLaughlan. Cameron A Gibson
PRESENTATION	*The Master then Presented Brother David Cummings with his Mark Master Mason Certificate.*
ALARM	*An Alarm was taken and admitted a large Deputation from Lodge Thistle and Rose No 73, headed on this occasion by their Master Brother David Agnew. The Master then welcomed the Visiting Deputation into the Lodge.*
ALARM	*An Alarm was taken and admitted the Deacons of Lodge Thistle and Rose No 73, along with Petition No 21 Mr Radu Razvan Chirila, Petition No 22, Mr Alastair Stewart Martin Reid ,Petition No 23 Mr Roney George Cook, who were then Initiated into Freemasonry by The Office Bearers of Lodge Thistle and Rose No 73,.*
OBLIGATION	*The Obligation was delivered by Brother David Agnew Master of Lodge Thistle and Rose No 73,*
	At the Completion of the Degree Brother Agnew returned the Maul to Brother McGroarty ,with a few well chosen words of thanks. The Office Bearers of Partick Saint Mary's Lodge resumed their Offices.

Secretary   10/   *Master*

27

Partick Saint Mary's Lodge.
Special Meeting ,
Wednesday 29th January 2020

Brother McGroarty thanked Lodge Thistle and Rose No 73,for an excellent rendition of the Entered Apprentice Degree..
Brother McGroarty then invited Brother Alex Ferguson Master of Lodge Kelvin Partick No 1207 to comment on tonight's Degree.
Brother Ferguson firstly thanked Partick Saint Mary's Lodge for the welcome extended to all the Visitors when entering the Temple.
Brother Ferguson stated all present had witnessed a fine Degree from Lodge Thistle and Rose No73.

NEXT MEETING   *The Master announced that the next meeting would be a Regular Meeting on Wednesday 5th February 2020 when Lodge Kelvin Partick No 1207 will confer the Fellowcraft Degree.*

CLOSED   *There being no further business the Lodge was closed in the Entered Apprentice Degree in due and ancient form and by prayer.*
The Master wished all a safe journey home and he hoped that they may return soon.

COLLECTION   *A collection was taken for the General Fund which raised £102.70. and for the Jewel and Regalia Fund £46.60.*

Prior to the commencement of the Meeting Brother Alan Cuthill P.M. explained Fire Evacuation Procedures and Safety Procedures should a fire occur.

Secretary   Master

Secretary   Master

Partick St Mary's Lodge
Regular Meeting
Wednesday 5th February 2020.

Regular Meeting
Masonic Temple
92 Dumbarton Road
Partick
Wednesday 5th February 2020.

OPENING — *A Regular Meeting of Partick Saint Mary's Lodge was held on the above date at 7.30pm. The Lodge was opened in due form and by prayer in the E.A Degree. The following Brethren were among those present at the opening*

PRESENT

Brother Andrew J. McGroarty.	*Master.*
Brother Alan Cuthill.	*I.P.M.*
Brother James Gallagher.	*W.S.W.*
Brother Harry Johnston D.M.	*Acting W.J.W.*
Brother Stanley MacLeod. P.M.	*S.D*
Brother Petros Karsaliakos.	*J.D* .
Brother Alex Morrison P.M.	*Acting I.G.*

And a total of 44 Brethren signed the Sederunt book.

WELCOME — *Welcoming the Brethren and the visitors into the Lodge, the Master then invited all Reigning and Past Masters for their assistance in the East.*

APOLOGIES — *Apologies were received from the following Brethren, Brothers John Gormly, P.M., Robert Angus P.M. Brothers Joshua W. Mitchell, Darren Grant, Donald MacKenzie, Peter Simpson, Alan Ordish, Jim Ordish, Jerome B Blanes, Cristian Urlea, W.J.W., Kevin McGowan, Andrew Buchanan, Graeme Clark, Keir Gorman, and James Hynds. Brothers Murray Hunter, Fred Christie, John Sharp, Cameron A. Gibson, Grant W. Mitchell, and Alex McLaughlin Honorary Members.*

MINUTES — *The Minute of Regular Meeting held on Wednesday 15th January 2020, which had been previously circulated by E-Mail, was approved and signed. The Minute of Special Meeting held on Wednesday 29th January 2020, which had been previously circulated by E-Mail, was approved and signed.*

SICK REPORT — *Brother Morrison reported that Brother Robert C. Short P.M. was making excellent progress after his recent Heart Operation and hoped to return to work in the near future. Brother Morrison intimated that Brother Malcolm Mackenzie has now returned home. Brother Morrison was informed that Brother Gorman had been admitted to Q.E.U.H. but was now home.*

CORRESPONDANCE — *Correspondence was received from :*
Grand Lodge Divine Service Glasgow Cathedral Sunday 29th March 2020.
Provincial Grand Lodge of Glasgow :Quiz Night Tue 31st March 2020.
John Adams Whist Wed 29th April 2020
Captain SpeirsGolf Competition.
1000 mile walk.
Invite to Lodge St George Helensburgh No 503, 150 years Celebrations on 4th April 2020.
Lodge Kelvin Partick No 1207 invite to their Centenary Celebrations on Saturday29/2/ 20 within Partick Burgh Hall.
Permission to erect their Past Masters Board received from Lodge Kelvin Partick No 1207.

Secretary — Graham A Agnew — 12/29 — *Master* — A McGroarty

Lodge Century No 1492: invite to Lecture on Monday 10th February.
Lodge Anima No 1223 invite to Installation Sat 8/2/20 at 4.00pm.

ACCOUNTS	*The Treasurer Brother Leighton said that there were no outstanding accounts. The Treasurer intimated that Lodge Diaries were on at hand.*

APPLICATIONS	*There were no applications received at the Secretary's desk.*

REPORTS	*Brother Hopes announced that he had visited 7 lodges since we last met. The Master thanked brother Hopes for undertaking these visitations .The Master thanked all those brethren who supported the Instruction Class held last Sunday (included were the 3 New initiates).*
Brother Cuthill proposed that we pay £55.00 as our annual fee for the W.D.L.A. This was Seconded by James S. Hartness P.M.

INTIMATIONS	*The Master asked for support from Brethren of the Lodge for Provincial Visits .*

ALARM	*An Alarm was taken and admitted a large Deputation from Lodge Kelvin Partick No 1207, which was headed on this occasion by their Master Brother Alexander Ferguson. The Master welcomed the Deputation into the Lodge.*

RECESS	*The Master adjourned the Lodge for a short period in order to prepare the Entered Apprentice. The Master resumed the Lodge. The Master then Passed the Lodge to the Second Square Degree of a Fellowcraft Freemason, after proving all to be Fellows of the Craft.*

PASSED	*The Master then presented Brother Ferguson with the Ceremonial Maul to enable Lodge Kelvin Partick to confer the Fellowcraft Degree. The Office Bearers of Partick St Mary's Lodge vacated their Offices in favour of the Office Bearers of Lodge Kelvin Partick No 1207.*

ALARM	*An Alarm was then taken and admitted Petition No 20, Brother Alasdair William Agnew, and Deacons of Lodge Kelvin Partick No 1207. Brother Agnew, an Entered Apprentice of this Lodge,was then Passed to the Rank of a Fellow of a Craft ,in a most proficient Manner by a team of Office Bearers from Lodge Kelvin Partick No 1207.*

OBLIGATION	*The Obligation was delivered by Brother Alexander Ferguson, Master of Lodge Kelvin Partick No 1207.*

CONCLUSION	*At the conclusion Brother Ferguson returned the Maul to Brother McGroarty with a few words of thanks. The Office Bearers of Partick Saint Mary's Lodge resumed their Offices, the Lodge was then reduced. Brother McGroarty then thanked Lodge Kelvin Partick No 1207. for an excellent rendition of the Fellowcraft Degree.*
The Master then invited Brother Adrain Beesley Master of Lodge Scotia No 178, to comment on to-nights Degree. Brother Beesley first thanked Partick Saint Mary's Lodge for the welcome extended to all on their arrival into the Temple. Brother Beesley then said that all present had witnessed a very special rendition of the Fellowcraft Degree.
The Master informed the Lodge that our next Meeting would be a Regular Meeting held on Wednesday 19th February 2020, which would be a M.M. Degree conferred by Lodge Galen No 1285.

CLOSED	*There being no further business the Lodge was Closed in the Entered Apprenticed Degree in due and ancient form and by prayer.*

COLLECTION	*For the General Fund £95.30.*
For the Jewel and Regalia Fund £ 43.80.

Secretary　　　　　　　　　12/　　　　　Master

Partick St Mary's Lodge
Regular Meeting
Wednesday 19th February 2020.

Regular Meeting
Masonic Temple
92 Dumbarton Road
Partick
Wednesday 19th February 2020.

OPENING   *A Regular Meeting of Partick Saint Mary's Lodge was held on the above date at 7.30 pm. The Lodge was opened in due form and by prayer in the E.A Degree. The following Brethren were among those present at the opening*

PRESENT

Brother Andrew J. McGroarty.	Master.
Brother Alan Cuthill.	I.P.M.
Brother James Gallagher.	W.S.W.
Brother Cristian Urlea.	W.J.W.
Brother Stanley MacLeod. P.M.	S.D
Brother Petros Karsaliakos.	J.D
Brother Andrew Buchanan.	I.G.

And a total of 51 Brethren signed the Sederunt book.

OBITUARY   *The Master informed the Brethren the Passing to the Grand Lodge above of Brother Alexander Harley Honorary Member, Brother Andrew Smith, Honorary Member, and Daniel McGowan brother of our Chaplain Brother Kevin McGowan.*
Brother Alan Cuthill then delivered fitting Eulogies for the aforementioned.
The Brethren were then upstanding as a mark of respect.

WELCOME   *Welcoming the Brethren and the visitors into the Lodge, the Master then invited all Reigning and Past Masters for their assistance in the East.*

APOLOGIES   *Apologies were received from the following Brethren,*
Brothers John Gormly, P.M., Robert Angus P.M. William Duff P.M., David W. Armstrong P.M., and Douglas Kowal P.M.
Brothers Joshua W. Mitchell, Darren Grant, Peter Simpson, Alan Ordish, Jim Ordish, Jerome B Blanes Mohammad Bachir. Douglas Smith.
Brothers Murray Hunter, Fred Christie, John Sharp, Ian Littlejohn Honorary Members.

MINUTES   *The Minute of Regular Meeting held on Wednesday 5th February 2020, having been previously circulated by E-Mail, was approved and signed.*

SICK REPORT *Brother Morrison reported that Brother Robert C. Short P.M. was making excellent progress after his recent Heart Operation and hoped to return to work in the near future.*

CORRESPONDANCE   *Correspondence was received from:*
Grand Lodge of Scotland J. Euan Edment Grand Secretary.
Grand Lodge Divine Service Sunday 29 March at Glasgow Cathedral.
Scottish Freemasonry Survey 2020.
Provincial Grand Lodge of Glasgow: Captain Speirs Golf Competition.

ACCOUNTS   *The Treasurer Brother Leighton stated that there were no outstanding Accounts.*
The Treasurer announced that Lodge Diaries were still on at hand.

APPLICATIONS   *There were no applications received at the Secretary's desk.*

REPORTS   *Brother Hopes advised that he had visited 7 Lodges since our last Meeting. The Master thanked Brother Hopes for putting the name of this Lodge to the fore .*

SECRETARY   32/20   MASTER

Partick St Mary's Lodge
Regular Meeting
Wednesday 5th February 2020.

Before closing the Lodge the Master invited all present to return for some Lodge Harmony. The Master wished all a safe journey and hoped the see them again in the near future.

SECRETARY *[signature]*   MASTER. *[signature]*

Prior to the commencement of the Meeting Brother Graeme D. Cameron P.M. explained Fire Evacuation Procedures and Safety Procedures should a Fire occur.

Partick St Mary's Lodge
Regular Meeting
Wednesday 19th February 2020.

INTIMATIONS The Master intimated that is was his intention to hold a Enquiry Meeting on Sunday 23rd February at 1.00pm followed by a Lodge of Instruction Class.

ALARM An Alarm was taken and admitted a large Deputation from Lodge Galen No 1285, which was headed on this occasion by their Master Brother Allan Dawson. The Master welcomed the Deputation into the Lodge.

RECESS The Master adjourned the Lodge for a short space of time, in order to prepare the fellowcraft. The Master thereafter resumed the Lodge.

MASTER MASON The Master then Raised the Lodge to the Third and High and Sublime Degree of a Master Mason after proving all present to be Master Masons. The Master then presented Brother Dawson with the Ceremonial Maul to enable Lodge Galen to confer the Master Mason Degree. The Office Bearers of Partick St Mary's Lodge vacated their Offices in favour of the Office Bearers of Lodge Galen No 1285.

ALARM An Alarm was then taken and admitted Petition No 19, Brother Alasdair William Agnew a Fellow craft of Partick Saint Mary's Lodge, and Deacons of Lodge Galen. No 1285. Brother Agnew was then Raised to the Rank of a Master Mason in a most proficient Manner by a team of Office Bearers from Lodge Galen No 1285.

OBLIGATION The Obligation was delivered by Brother David F, Quinn, Past Master of Lodge Galen No 1285.

CONCLUSION At the conclusion Brother Dawson returned the Ceremonial Maul to Brother McGroarty with a few words of thanks. The Office Bearers of Partick Saint Mary's resumed their Offices, the Lodge was then reduced to the Entered Apprentice Degree. Brother McGroarty then thanked Lodge Galen for an excellent rendition of the Master Mason Degree.
The Master then invited Brother Alexander Ferguson Master of Lodge Kelvin Partick No 1207, to comment on to-nights Degree. Brother Ferguson first thanked Partick Saint Mary's Lodge for the welcome extended to all on their arrival into the Temple. Brother Ferguson then stated that all present had witnessed a very special rendition of the Master Mason Degree.

PRESENTATION The Master then presented Brother Morrison with his 50 year Jewel which had been overlooked by the Lodge.
The Master informed the Lodge that our next Meeting would be the Grand Lodge of Glasgow Visitation.
Dinner suites to be worn by Senior Office Bearers.

SECRETARY   33/20   MASTER

CLOSED   *There being no further business the Lodge was Closed in the Entered Apprenticed Degree in due and ancient form and by prayer.*

COLLECTION   *For the General Fund £112.50.*
For the Jewel and Regalia Fund £ 48.30.

Before closing the Lodge the Master invited all present to return for some Lodge Harmony. The Master wished all those not staying for \Harmony he wish a safe journey and hoped the see them again in the near future.

SECRETARY   MASTER.

Prior to the commencement of the Meeting Brother Graeme D. Cameron P.M. explained Fire Evacuation Procedures and Safety Procedures should a Fire occur.

SECRETARY   35/20   MASTER

WGP WRSDAY 04 MARCH 2020

~~Thursday, 05 March 2020~~, 92 Dumbarton Road, Glasgow, G11 6NX

Substitute Provincial Grand Master, Brother Duncan McFadyen, accompanied by a deputation of Office Bearers and Stewards from the Provincial Grand Lodge of Glasgow visited Partick St. Mary's Lodge, No. 117 on the above date and found the Lodge to be working in conformity with the Constitution and Laws of the Grand Lodge of Scotland.

All Dues to Grand Lodge and Provincial Grand Lodge have been paid.

~~Provincial Grand Master~~...... Duncan D. McA. McFadyen SPGM

Acting Provincial Grand Secretary:........................

35/20

SECRETARY,   MASTER.

During the Meeting Brother Graeme D. Cameron P.M. D.O.C. explained Fire Evacuations Procedures and Safety Procedures should a Fire occur.

Partick Saint Mary's Lodge,
Enquiry Committee,
Sunday 23rd February 2020.

Enquiry Committee Meeting,
Masonic Temple,
92 Dumbarton Road,
Partick.
Sunday 23rd February 2020.

OPENING   *A Meeting of the above Committee took place on Sunday 23nd February 2020, at 14.00.*

PRESENT

Brother Alan Cuthill	*I.P.M.*
Brother James Gallagher	*W.S.W.*
Brother Graham A. Agnew P.M.	*Secretary.*
Brother John McK. Leighton	*Treasurer.*

PM's present Brothers, Graeme D. Cameron, Stanley MacLeod.

APOLOGIES *Brother Andrew J. McGroarty, Master Brother Cristian Urlea. W.J.W.*

Before the Meeting Commenced Brother Agnew informed the Committee that the Lodge applied to the Grand Lodge of Scotland for a Dispensation Certificate which has now been granted.

PETITION 24 *An Application for Initiation into Freemasonry having been read on Wednesday 19th February 2020, on behalf of Petition 24 Mr. Sultan Suhail Musa, 4/1/2000, Student, Unviversity of Strathclyde.*
Place of Birth Oman, Muscat
Residing at 1-3 Thurso Street Glasgow G11 6PC.
Proposed by Brother Mohammad Bachir.
Seconded by Brother Stanley MacLeod PM., and in keeping with Grand Lodge Law No 168 the Applicant, his Proposer and Seconder, both being in good standing, were this afternoon interviewed. All having given satisfactory answers to the question asked of them, The Applicant was advised of the procedure which would ensue.

Secretary

Master.

Secretary   39 / 20   Master

Partick Saint Mary's Lodge No 117
Enquiry Committee Meeting
Wednesday 11th December 2019.

Enquiry Committee Meeting,
Masonic Temple ,
92 Dumbarton Road ,
Partick.
Thursday 18th March 2020.

OPENING   *A Meeting of the above Committee took place on Sunday 14th March at 7.00pm.*

PRESENT
Brother Andrew J. McGroarty.	*Master.*
Brother James Gallagher.	*W.S.W.*
Brother Cristian Urlea.	*W.J.W.*
Brother Graham A Agnew. P.M.	*Secretary.*
Brother John McK. Leighton.	*Treasurer.*

PM's present Brothers Stanley MacLeod, Alan Cuthill.

APOLOGIES

PETITION 26 *An Application for Initiation into Freemasonry having been read on Wednesday 4th March 2020, on behalf of Petition 26 Mr. Martin Richard Bateman, D.O.B.18/9/1994, Student Glasgow Unviversary*
Place of Birth Stafford, England, Nationality British.
Residing at 53 Avenuepark Street Maryhill, Glasgow G20 8LN. 7UE.
Proposed by Brother Alan Cuthill P.M.
Seconded by Brother Stanley Macleod ,and in keeping with Grand Lodge Law No 168 the Applicant ,his Proposer and Seconder ,both being in good standing, were this evening interviewed. All having given satisfactory answers to the question asked of them, The Applicant was advised of the procedure which would ensue.

There being no further business the Meeting was Closed with a vote of thanks to the Chair.

SECRETARY   MASTER.

Secretary   Master

Regular Meeting
Masonic Temple
92 Dumbarton Road
Wednesday 4th March 2020

OPENING *A Regular Meeting of Partick Saint Mary's Lodge was held on the above date at 7.15 pm. The Lodge was opened in due form and by prayer in the E.A Degree. The following Brethren were among those present at the opening*

PRESENT

Brother Andrew S. McGroarty.	*Master.*
Brother Alan Cuthill.	*I.P.M.*
Brother James Gallagher.	*W. S. W.*
Brother Cristian Urlea.	*W.J.W.*
Brother Petros Kalsaliakos.	*S.D.*
Brother Stanley MacLeod. P.M.	*J.D.*
Brother Andrew Buchanan.	*I.G.*

and a total of 66 Brethren signed the Sederunt.,

APOLOGIES *Apologies were received from the following Brethren: Robert Angus P.M. John Gormly. P.M. Robert C. Short P.M.*

Brothers Darren Grant, Joshua W. Mitchell, George De Feyter, Dale Cutless, Keir Gorman, George Ladas.

Hon Mem's Fred Christie, Grant W. Mitchell, John Sharp.

WELCOME *The Master having welcoming the Brethren and the visitors into the Lodge, he then invited Reigning and Past Masters to give him their assistance in the East.*

SICK REPORT *Brother Alex Morrison Almoner stated that there was nothing to report.*

MINUTES The Minute of the last Regular Meeting held on 19th February 2020, which had already been circulated by E-mail was approved and signed.

CORRESPONDENCE Correspondence: There was Correspondence: received:
Grand Lodge of Scotland :Amendment to Law 126.
Advice on Corona Virus situation Health issues..
Vacancy for IT Manager.
Provincial Grand Lodge :Essay Competition 2020.
10 sponsored mile walk

ACCOUNTS Bro John Leighton Treasurer said that there were outstanding Accounts.

APPLICATIONS Mr Martin Richard Bakewell. D.O.B.18/9/1994. P.O.B. Stafford. British, Student, Glasgow University.
Residing at 53 Avenuepark Street, Maryhill, Glasgow G20 8LN.
Proposed John McKay Leighton. Seconded Stanley MacLeod P.M.

SECRETARY

MASTER

38/20

Mr Vincent Roger Amsoms. D.O.B. 22/1/1986. P.O.B. Ankora, Mali. Hospitality Manager. Residing at 1083 Sauchiehall Street, Glasgow. G3 7UE.
Proposed by Brother, Alan Cuthill P.M.   Seconded by Brother Stanley MacLeod P.M.

REPORTS   The Master thanked all who accompanied him on the various Provincial Visitations.

INTIMATIONS   The Master made the following Intimations
Divine Service Sunday 8th March, Partick South Church 2pm for 2.30pm
Lodge Knightswood No 1445 PGL Visitation Friday 6th March 2020 at 19.30.
Visit to Lodge Tower No 1523 on 13th March to Confer an Exemplification of the E. A. Degree.

ALARM   An Alarm was taken and admitted a large and distinguished Deputation from our Sister Lodges, the Deputation was headed by Brother Kenneth J. Sinclair, Master, Lodge Tower No 1523, and after welcoming the Deputation into the Lodge, the Master then invited Masters Past and Present to accompany him in the East.

PRESENTATION   Brother Neill then presented a Clock, to the Lodge from Lodge Western to mark our 250 Anniversary Celebrations Brother McGroarty thanked Lodge Western for this kind gesture.

ALARM   An alarm was taken and admitted Brother Secretary and Brother Treasurer, who had previously retired.

ALARM   A final alarm admitted a Deputation from The Provincial Grand Lodge of Glasgow, this being headed by Brother Duncan D. McA. McFadyen, Worshipful Substitute Provincial Grand Master.

MALLET   The Master then welcomed the Deputation into the Lodge and then presented Brother Duncan D. McA. McFadyen with the Mallet, pledging the Lodge's fealty to the Provincial Grand Lodge of Glasgow and through that august body to the Grand Lodge of Scotland. Brother Duncan D. McA. McFadyen thanked the Master and for the Lodge's pledge of fealty. The S.P.G.M. then introduced his Deputation to the Brethren. The Provincial D.O.C. then requested that the Office Bearers of Partick Saint Mary's Lodge vacate their offices in favour of the Office Bearers and Stewards of Provincial Grand Lodge of Glasgow.

The. S.P.G.M. Brother Duncan D. McA. McFadyen, then reviewed the workings of the Lodge during the previous year and intimated that he had caused a clear minute to be inserted in the Lodge Minute book. He called on the Acting P.G.L. Secretary to read it.

Brother Duncan D. McA. McFadyen congratulated those Brethren who had supported the Master during this year under review in particular Bro Graham A. Agnew, P.M. John Leighton and Alex Morrison P.M..

MALLET   Brother Duncan D. McA. McFadyen then returned the Mallet, to the Master of the Lodge Office Bearer's and Stewards of P.G.L. vacated their offices in favour of the Office .Bearers of Partick Saint Mary's Lodge. The Master then asked Brother Alan Cuthill I.P.M. to responded to the remarks made by S.P.G.M. The I.P.M. thanked the Provincial Grand Lodge of Glasgow for giving the Lodge a Clear minute. The I.PM. then thanked all who had supported him during this Special year in our Lodge's History. and to the Brethren of the Lodge for affording the great honour of being Master during our 250 Celebrations.

RETIRAL   The Provincial Grand Lodge of Glasgow then retired from the Lodge, after being invited to return for Lodge Hospitality. This request was gratefully accepted by the S.P.G.M. Brother Duncan D. McA. McFadyen.

CLOSED   There being no further competent business the Lodge was closed in the E.A. Degree, in Due and Ancient form and by prayer.

COLLECTION   Collection for the Lodge Benevolent Fund £187.00

Enquiry Committee Meeting,
Masonic Temple ,
92 Dumbarton Road ,
Partick.
Sunday 14th March 2020.

OPENING   *A Meeting of the above Committee took place on Sunday 14th March at 2.00pm.*

PRESENT   *Brother Andrew J. McGroarty.*   *Master.*
Brother James Gallagher   *W.S.W.*
Brother Graham A Agnew P.M.   *Secretary.*
Brother John McK. Leighton   *Treasurer.*
PM's present Brothers Stanley MacLeod, Alan Cuthill.

APOLOGIES *Brother Cristain Urlea W.J.W.*

PETITION 25 *An Application for Initiation into Freemasonry having been read on Wednesday 4th March 2020, on behalf of Petition 25 Mr. Vincent Roger Amsoms , D.O.B.22/1/1986, Hotel General Manager, Place of Birth Ankora Turkey, Nationality Turkish.*
Residing at Flat1/2 1083 Sauchiehall Street Glasgow G3 7UE.
Proposed by Brother Alan Cuthill P.M.
Seconded by Brother Stanley Macleod ,and in keeping with Grand Lodge Law No 168 the Applicant ,his Proposer and Seconder ,both being in good standing, were this evening interviewed. All having given satisfactory answers to the question asked of them, The Applicant was advised of the procedure which would ensue.

There being no further business the Meeting was Closed with a vote of thanks to the Chair.

SECRETARY   MASTER.

Secretary   Master

Enquiry Committee Meeting,
Masonic Temple ,
92 Dumbarton Road ,
Partick.
Sunday 22nd December 2019.

OPENING   *A Meeting of the above Committee took place on Sunday 22nd December 2019, at 14.00.*

PRESENT

Brother Andrew J. McGroarty.	*Master.*
Brother Alan Cuthill	*I.P.M.*
Brother James Gallagher	*W.S.W.*
Brother Graham A Agnew P.M.	*Secretary.*
Brother John McK. Leighton	*Treasurer.*

PM's present Brothers, Graeme D. Cameron, Stanley MacLeod.

APOLOGIES   *Brother Cristian Urlea. W.J.W.*

PETITION 19   *An Application for Initiation into Freemasonry having been read on Wednesday 4th September 2019, on behalf of Petition 19 Mr. Florion Stefan Niederseer, D.O.B.21/9/1998, Student , Unviversity of Glasgow, Place of Birth Salzburg, Austria, Nationality Austrain. Residing at 20 Cecil Street Glasgow. G12 8RH.*

Proposed by Brother Alan Cuthill P.M. Seconded by Brother Stanley MacLeod P.M. and in keeping with Grand Lodge Law No 168 the Applicant, his Proposer and Seconder, both being in good standing, were this afternoon interviewed. All having given satisfactory answers to the question asked of them, The Applicant was advised of the procedure which would ensue.

BALLOT TO BE HELD OVER UNTIL MARCH,(Applicants request)

Secretary

Master.

Secretary   42   Master

Partick Saint Mary's Lodge No 117
Regular Meeting
1st September 2021.

Regular Meeting
Masonic Temple
92 Dumbarton Road
Partick
Wednesday 1st September 2021.

OPENING   *A Regular Meeting of Partick Saint Mary's Lodge was held within the Harmony Room   on the above date at 7.30 pm. The Lodge was opened in due form and by prayer in the E.A Degree. The following Brethren were among those present at the opening .*

PRESENT

Brother Andrew S. McGroarty.	*Master.*
Brother Alan Cuthill.	*I.P.M.*
Brother James Gallagher.	*W. S. W.*
Brother Cristian Urlea.	*W.J.W.*
Brother Petros Kalsaliakos.	*S.D.*
Brother Stanley MacLeod. P.M.	*J.D.*
Brother Andrew Buchanan.	*I.G.*

and a total 22 Brethren signed the Sederunt.,

APOLOGIES   *Apologies were received from the following Brethren: Robert Angus P.M. John Gormly P.M. Robert C. Short P.M. David Armstrong P.M. and William Duff P.M.*
Brothers: Joshua W. Mitchell, Dale Cutless, George Ladas, Robert McKelvie.
Hon Mem 's, Grant W. Mitchell, John Sharp.

OBITURIES   *The Master said that during the last 18 Months absence due to Subject Covid 19 restrictions there were 6 Brethren of the Lodge who had Passed to the Grand Lodge Above; Brothers John Hutchison who was resident in New Zealand , Brother Jim Craig M.M.*
Brothers Keir Gorman, Alexander Palmer, Stewart Murray all Affiliate Members
Brother Alexander Gibson P.M. 18 Honorary Member.
The Master asked the Brethren to be up standing as a token of respect to these well respected Brethren.

WELCOME   *The Master welcoming the Brethren and the visitors back into the Lodge after our enforced break and hope all were safe and well.*

SICK REPORT   *Bro Alex Morrison Almoner said that he had visited Brother Lewis Halliburton who was in poor health and would keep the Lodge informed of Brother Halliburton's health.*

MINUTES   *The Minute of the last Regular Meeting held on 4th September 2020, which had already been circulated by E-mail was approved and signed.*
The Minutes of the last Enquiry Meetings held on 4th September 2020, and Wednesday 19th February were read and a Ballot took place for Mr Martin Richard Bateman.
The Brother Secretary explained why four Minutes were read and (only one Balloted,) were was approved and signed.

BALLOT   *A Ballot took place on behalf of Petition No 26 Mr Martin Richard Bateman and found to be clear.*
Brother Agnew said that Mr Bateman will be advise when he will be Initiated.

CORRESPONDENCE   *Correspondence: There was Correspondence: received:*
Grand Lodge of Scotland : Several letters concerning Covid 19.
2021 Grand Lodge Calendar.
Poppy Scotland.
Provincial Grand Lodge; Donation of disused tablet devices.
Several Administration Letters.
Lodge H.L.I./ The Royal Highland Fusiliers Moving out of Dumbarton Road.

APPLICATIONS   *Brother Secretary said that there were 11 Gentlemen seeking to join Partick Saint Mary's Lodge (list of Candidates enclosed). Brother Secretary said that he had written to all of them giving a Date and Time when to attend their Enquiry.*

REPORTS   *The Master thanked all for their attendance here to-night.*
The Master said that during lockdown the Lodge has undergone several changes.
The Harmony Room Painted, and new light fittings.
A new Gents Toilet built on the Middle Floor.
The Lodge Room, painted new carpeting, new Lodge Carpet, and all the Electrics checked and certified.

SECRETARY   */21*   *MASTER*

Partick Saint Mary's Lodge No 117
Regular Meeting
1st September 2021.

ACCOUNTS	*Brother Leighton asked the Lodge to Pass the Accounts for 2019 -2020. The Members of Partick Saint Mary's Lodge were then given a copy of these Accounts. Brother Leighton then when over the Expenditure and Income and asked if there were any questions. Brother Morrison gave a summary of the Benevolent Fund. The Master then asked for a Proposer and seconder of these Accounts. Brother Hartness, Proposed and Brother Graeme Cameron Seconded these Accounts.*

The Master thanked Brother Leighton for the careful and diligent recording and preparing of the Lodge Accounts for the last 17 years.

CLOSED   *There being no further competent business the Lodge was closed in the E.A. Degree, in due and ancient form and by prayer.*

COLLECTION   *Collections for; General Fund   £74.00.*
                          Jewel and Regalia   £35.00.

After a short refreshment Brother Petros Karsaliakos gave a very informative talk on the meaning of several Masonic words The Master then thanked Brother Karsaliakos for a very thoughtful talk and the time taken to compile this interesting lecture.

SECRETARY.   MASTER.

SECRETARY   **2** /21   MASTER

Partick Saint Mary's Lodge,
Enquiry Committee,
Sunday 5th September 2021.

Enquiry Committee Meeting,
Masonic Temple,
92 Dumbarton Road,
Partick.
Sunday 5th September 2021.

OPENING   *A Meeting of the above Committee took place on Sunday 5th September 2021, at 13.00.*

PRESENT

Brother Alan Cuthill	*I.P.M.*
Brother Cristian Urlea.	*W.S.W.*
Brother Graham A. Agnew P.M.	*Secretary.*

PM's present Brothers, Graeme D. Cameron, Stanley MacLeod.

APOLOGIES *Brother Andrew J. McGroarty, Master, Brother Johm McK. Leighton Treasurer. Brother James Gallagher. W.J.W.*

PETITION 26 *An Application for Initiation into Freemasonry having been read on Wednesday 1st September 2021, on behalf of Petition 26 Mr Bruce Iain Jardine   D.O.B ,13/11/1975, Recruitment Manager, P.O.B. Birmingham. Residing at 65 Wilton Street Glasgow G20 6RD.*
Proposed by Brother Graeme D. Cameron P.M. .
Seconded by Brother Stanley MacLeod PM., and in keeping with Grand Lodge Law No 168 the Applicant, his Proposer and Seconder, both being in good standing, were this afternoon interviewed. All having given satisfactory answers to the question asked of them, The Applicant was advised of the procedure which would ensue.

PETITION 27 *An Application for Initiation into Freemasonry having been read on Wednesday 1st September 2021, on behalf of Petition 27 Mr Barry Kane , D.O.B ,10/6/1991, Marketing Manager, P.O.B. Glasgow .*
Residing at 37 Cedar Street Glasgow G20 7NR..
Proposed by Brother Graeme. Cameron P.M.
Seconded by Brother Graham A. Agnew P.M., and in keeping with Grand Lodge Law No 168 the Applicant, his Proposer and Seconder, both being in good standing, were this afternoon interviewed. All having given satisfactory answers to the question asked of them, The Applicant was advised of the procedure which would ensue.

Secretary   Master.

Michael Mitchell Cowley

DOB 12/12/1975

11 Fischer Gardens
Paisley
Renfrewshire
PA1 2ST

Occupation : Director MCS Safety Systems

Nationality: British

Proposed: Alan Cuthill P.M.
Seconded John Leighton

Nesi Bahar

DOB 28/01/1996

23 Rosevale Street
Partick
Glasgow
G11 6EL

Occupation : Doctor

Nationality: Italian

Proposed: Alan Cuthill P.M.
Seconded: John Leighton

Christian Gotts

DOB: 03/07/1991

15 Keith Court
Partick
Glasgow
G11 6AW

Occupation: Doctor

Nationality: British

Proposed: Alan Cuthill P.M.
Seconded: Stanley MacLeod P.M.

Bruce Iain Jardine

13/11/1975

65 Wilton Street
North Kelvinside
Glasgow
G20 6RD

Occupation: Recruitment Manager

Nationality:British

Proposed: Graeme D. Cameron P.M.
Seconded: Stanley MacLeod P.M.

Barry Kane

DOB: 10/06/1991

37 Cedar Street
Glasgow
G20 7NX

Occupation: Marketing Manager

Nationality: British

Willikens Costa De Santos

17/12/1972

3/2, 9 Fordyce Street
Partick
Glasgow
G11 5PF

Occuaption: Childcare Assistant

Nationality: Brazilian

Proposed: Graeme D. Cameron P.M
Seconded: Stanley MacLeod P.M,

Mark Andrew McLymont

DOB: 03/02/1981

3/2, 28 Kenoway Drive
Glasgow
G11 7NY

Occupation: Technical Operator

Nationality: British

Proposed: Alan Cuthill P.M.
Seconded: Stanley MacLeod P.M.

Stephen Wallace

DOB: 16/05/1994

2/2, 16 Guthrie Street
Wyndford
Glasgow
G20 8DL

Occupation: BarStaff

Nationality: British

Proposer: Graeme D. Cameron P.M.
Seconded Stanley MacLeod P.M.

Partick Saint Mary's Lodge,
Enquiry Committee,
Sunday 5th September 2021.

Enquiry Committee Meeting,
Masonic Temple,
92 Dumbarton Road,
Partick.
Sunday 5th September 2021.

OPENING   *A Meeting of the above Committee took place on Sunday 5th September 2021, at 13.00.*

PRESENT

Brother Alan Cuthill	*I.P.M.*
Brother Cristian Urlea.	*W.S.W.*
Brother Graham A. Agnew P.M.	*Secretary.*

PM's present Brothers, Graeme D. Cameron, Stanley MacLeod.

APOLOGIES *Brother Andrew J. McGroarty, Master, Brother Johm McK. Leighton Treasurer. Brother James Gallagher. W.J.W.*

PETITION 26 *An Application for Initiation into Freemasonry having been read on Wednesday 1st September 2021, on behalf of Petition 26 Mr Bruce Iain Jardine D.O.B ,13/11/1975, Recruitment Manager, P.O.B. Birmingham. Residing at 65 Wilton Street Glasgow G20 6RD.*
Proposed by Brother Graeme D. Cameron P.M. .
Seconded by Brother Stanley MacLeod PM., and in keeping with Grand Lodge Law No 168 the Applicant, his Proposer and Seconder, both being in good standing, were this afternoon interviewed. All having given satisfactory answers to the question asked of them, The Applicant was advised of the procedure which would ensue.

PETITION 27 *An Application for Initiation into Freemasonry having been read on Wednesday 1st September 2021, on behalf of Petition 27 Mr Barry Kane , D.O.B ,10/6/1991, Marketing Manager, P.O.B. Glasgow . Residing at 37 Cedar Street Glasgow G20 7NR..*
Proposed by Brother Graeme. Cameron P.M.
Seconded by Brother Graham A. Agnew P.M., and in keeping with Grand Lodge Law No 168 the Applicant, his Proposer and Seconder, both being in good standing, were this afternoon interviewed. All having given satisfactory answers to the question asked of them, The Applicant was advised of the procedure which would ensue.

Secretary Graham A Agnew   *Master.*

Secretary   49/21   Master

Partick Saint Mary's Lodge,
Enquiry Committee,
Wednesday 1th September 2021.
SUNDAY.

Enquiry Committee Meeting,
Masonic Temple,
92 Dumbarton Road,
Partick.
Sunday 5th September 2021.

OPENING *A Meeting of the above Committee took place on Sunday 5th September 2021, at 13.00.*

PRESENT

Brother Alan Cuthill   *I.P.M.*
Brother Cristian Urlea.   *W.S.W.*
Brother Graham A. Agnew P.M.   *Secretary.*
PM's present Brothers, Graeme D. Cameron, Stanley MacLeod.

APOLOGIES *Brother Andrew J. McGroarty, Master, Brother Johm McK. Leighton Treasurer. Brother James Gallagher. W.J.W.*

PETITION 26 *An Application for Initiation into Freemasonry having been read on Wednesday 1st September 2021, on behalf of Petition 26 Mr Bruce Iain Jardine D.O.B ,13/11/1975, Recruitment Manager, P.O.B. Birmingham. Residing at 65 Wilton Street Glasgow G20 6RD.*
Proposed by Brother Graeme D. Cameron P.M. .
Seconded by Brother Stanley MacLeod P.M., and in keeping with Grand Lodge Law No 168 the Applicant, his Proposer and Seconder, both being in good standing, were this afternoon interviewed. All having given satisfactory answers to the question asked of them, The Applicant was advised of the procedure which would ensue.

PETITION 27 *An Application for Initiation into Freemasonry having been read on Wednesday 1st September 2021, on behalf of Petition 27 Mr Barry Kane , D.O.B ,10/6/1991, Marketing Manager, P.O.B. Glasgow . Residing at 37 Cedar Street Glasgow G20 7NR..*
Proposed by Brother Graeme. Cameron P.M.
Seconded by Brother Graham A. Agnew P.M., and in keeping with Grand Lodge Law No 168 the Applicant, his Proposer and Seconder, both being in good standing, were this afternoon interviewed. All having given satisfactory answers to the question asked of them, The Applicant was advised of the procedure which would ensue.

Secretary   Master.

Secretary   4/21   Master

Partick Saint Mary's Lodge,
Enquiry Committee,
Wednesday 15th September 2021.

PETITION 29 An Application for Initiation into Freemasonry having been read on
Wednesday 1st September 2021, on behalf of Petition 29 Mr Willikens Costa
Dos Santos D.O.B ,17/12/1972, Child Care Assistant , P.O.B. Brazil .
Residing at 3/2 9 Fordyce Street, Partick, Glasgow G11 5PF.
Proposed by Brother Graeme D. Cameron P.M. .
Seconded by Brother Stanley MacLeod PM., and in keeping with Grand Lodge
Law No 168 the Applicant, his Proposer and Seconder, both being in good
standing, were this afternoon interviewed. All having given satisfactory answers
to the question asked of them, The Applicant was advised of the procedure which
would ensue.

PETITION 30 An Application for Initiation into Freemasonry having been read on
Wednesday 1st September 2021, on behalf of Petition 30 Mr Mark Andrew
McClymont, D.O.B ,3/2/1981, Technical Operator., P.O.B. Bellshill .
Residing at 3/2 28 Kenoway Drive ,Glasgow G11 7NY.
Proposed by Brother Alan Cuthill P.M.
Seconded by Brother Stanley MacLeod PM., and in keeping with Grand Lodge
Law No 168 the Applicant, his Proposer and Seconder, both being in good
standing, were this afternoon interviewed. All having given satisfactory answers
to the question asked of them, The Applicant was advised of the procedure which
would ensue.

The Meeting was closed with a vote of thanks to the Chair.

Secretary   5/21   Master

Partick Saint Mary's Lodge
Regular Meeting
15th September 2021.

Regular Meeting

Masonic Temple

92 Dumbarton Road

Partick

Wednesday 15th September 2021.

OPENING	A Regular Meeting of Partick Saint Mary's Lodge was held within the Harmony Room on the above date at 7.30 pm. The Lodge was opened in due form and by prayer in the E.A Degree. The following Brethren were among those present at the opening.

PRESENT

Brother Andrew S. McGroarty.	Master.
Brother Alan Cuthill.	I.P.M.
Brother James Gallagher.	W. S. W.
Brother Cristian Urea.	W.J.W.
Brother Petros Karsaliakos.	S.D.
Brother Stanley MacLeod. P.M.	J.D.
Brother Andrew Buchanan.	I.G.

and a total 22 Brethren signed the Sederunt.,

APOLOGIES   Apologies were received from the following Brethren: William Duff P.M. John Gormly P.M. Douglas Kowal P.M.
Brothers: Joshua W. Mitchell, Dale Cutless, George Ladas, Robert McKelvie. Alasdair W. Agnew, George De Feyter, Jim Craig, Jerome Blanes, Douglas Smith,
Hon Mem 's, Grant W. Mitchell, John Sharp.

WELCOME   The Master welcoming the Brethren to our Regular Meeting and in particular Brother David Best. The Master also welcomed brothers who were attending their first Meeting Since the Lockdown had been lifted..

SICK REPORT Bro Alex Morrison Almoner said that he had nothing to report.

MINUTES   The Minute of the last Regular Meeting held on 1st September 2021, which had already been circulated by E-mail was approved and signed.

The Minutes of the last Enquiry Meetings held on 5th September 2021, and Wednesday 15th September 2021, for Petition 26,Mr Bruce Iain Jardine , Petition 27, Mr Barry Kane, Petition 29 Mr Willekens Cost Dos Santos, Petition 30, Mr Mark Andrew McClymont, Petition 32, Dr Nesi Bahar .

BALLOT   A Ballot took place on behalf of the above Petitions. It was agreed that these be taken On Bloc. and found to be clear.

AFFILIATION The Minutes of the last Enquiry Meetings held on 12th September 2021, on behalf of Petition No 31 Stephen Wallace M.M. Universities of Staffordshire Lodge, No 9907 E.C. Brother Secretary said that he would write to Grand Secretary asking if he would write to the U.G. L.E for clarification.

CORRESPONDENCE Brother Secretary said that no Correspondence had been received .

1/22

Partick Saint Mary's Lodge
Regular Meeting
15th September 2021.

APPLICATIONS   *Brother Secretary said that there were 2 Gentlemen seeking to join Partick Saint Mary's Lodge ; Mr Adermane Laban D.O.B. 29/4/1986 An Interpreter P.O.B. Chad.*

Residing at 59 Union Street Glasgow G1 3RB.

Proposer Brother Alan Cuthill P.M.

Seconder Brother Stanley MacLeod P.M.

Donald Eugene Spencer, D.O.B.30/5/1993, Student Glasgow University, P.O.B. California United States of America.

Residing at 1/1 65 Avenue Park Street Glasgow G20   8LU.

Proposer Brother Alan Cuthill P.M.

Seconder Brother Stanley MacLeod P.M.

Brother Secretary was then asked to arrange an Enquiry Meeting for these two gentlemen.

CLOSED   *There being no further competent business the Lodge was closed in the E.A. Degree, in due and ancient form and by prayer.*

COLLECTION *Collections for; General Fund   £74.00.*
Jewel and Regalia   £35.00.

After a short refreshment Brother Alan Cuthill, I.P.M. gave a very informative talk on Masonic Literature several of these Masonic books are in the Lodge Library words   The Master then thanked Brother Cuthill for another thoughtful and interesting Lecture as per usual from Brother Cuthill

SECRETARY.

MASTER. *A M Gearty*

2/22

Partick Saint Mary's Lodge,
Enquiry Committee,
Sunday 12th September 2021.

Enquiry Committee Meeting,
Masonic Temple,
92 Dumbarton Road,
Partick.
Sunday 12th September 2021.

OPENING   *A Meeting of the above Committee took place on Sunday 12th September 2021, at 14.00.*

PRESENT

Brother Andrew J. McGroarty,	*Master.*
Brother Alan Cuthill	*I.P.M.*
Brother Cristian Urlea.	*W.S.W.*
Brother James Gallagher.	*W.J.W.*
Brother Graham A. Agnew P.M.	*Secretary.*
Brother John McK. Leighton.	*Treasurer.*

PM's present Brothers, Graeme D. Cameron, Stanley MacLeod.

APOLOGIES *Brother Cristian Urlea.*   *W.S.W.*

PETITION 31 *An Application for Affiliation into Partick Saint Mary's Lodge having been read on Wednesday 1st September 2021.*
Brother Stephen Wallace, M.M. Universities Lodge of Staffordshire No 9907 English Constitution.
Residing at 2/2 16 Guthrie Street Wyndford Glasgow G20 8DL.
Brother Secretary to write to Grand Secretary to get approval from Grand Lodge of Scotland to proceed with this application.
Proposed by Brother Graeme D. Cameron P.M.
Seconded by Brother Stanley MacLeod PM., and in keeping with Grand Lodge Law No 168 the Applicant, his Proposer and Seconder, both being in good standing, were this afternoon interviewed. All having given satisfactory answers to the question asked of them, The Applicant was advised of the procedure which would ensue.

There being no further business the Meeting was Closed and a vote of thanks to the Chair.

Secretary   Master

Partick Saint Mary's Lodge,
Enquiry Committee,
Wednesday 15th September 2021.

Enquiry Committee Meeting,
Masonic Temple,
92 Dumbarton Road,
Partick.
Wednesday 15th September 2021.

OPENING *A Meeting of the above Committee took place on Wednesday 15th September 2021, at 18.30.*

PRESENT

Brother Andrew J. McGroarty,	*Master.*
Brother Alan Cuthill	*I.P.M.*
Brother Cristian Urlea.	*W.S.W.*
Brother James Gallagher.	*W.J.W.*
Brother Graham A. Agnew P.M.	*Secretary.*
Brother John McK. Leighton.	*Treasurer.*

PM's present Brothers, Graeme D. Cameron, Stanley MacLeod.

APOLOGIES

PETITION 32 *An Application for Initiation into Freemasonry having been read on Wednesday 1st September 2021, on behalf of Petition 32 Dr Nesi Bahar D.O.B ,28/01/1995, Doctor, P.O.B. Istanbul , Turkey.*
Residing at 23 Rosevale Street Partick Glasgow G11 6EL.
Proposed by Brother Alan Cuthill P.M.
Seconded by Brother Stanley MacLeod PM., and in keeping with Grand Lodge Law No 168 the Applicant, his Proposer and Seconder, both being in good standing, were this afternoon interviewed. All having given satisfactory answers to the question asked of them, The Applicant was advised of the procedure which would ensue.

The Meeting was Closed with a vote of thank to the Chair

Secretary   63/21   Master

Partick Saint Mary's Lodge,
Enquiry Committee,
Sunday 12th September 2021.

Enquiry Committee Meeting,
Masonic Temple,
92 Dumbarton Road,
Partick.
Wednesday 15th September 2021.

OPENING   *A Meeting of the above Committee took place on Wednesday 15th September 2021, at 18.30.*

PRESENT

Brother Andrew J. McGroarty,	*Master.*
Brother Alan Cuthill	*I.P.M.*
Brother Cristian Urlea.	*W.S.W.*
Brother James Gallagher.	*W.J.W.*
Brother Graham A. Agnew P.M.	*Secretary.*
Brother John McK. Leighton.	*Treasurer.*

PM's present Brothers, Graeme D. Cameron, Stanley MacLeod.

APOLOGIES

PETITION 32 *An Application for Initiation into Freemasonry having been read on Wednesday 1st September 2021, on behalf of Petition 32 Dr Nesi Bahar D.O.B ,28/01/1995, Doctor, P.O.B. Istanbul , Turkey.*
Residing at 23 Rosevale Street Partick Glasgow G11 6EL.
Proposed by Brother Alan Cuthill P.M.
Seconded by Brother Stanley MacLeod PM., and in keeping with Grand Lodge Law No 168 the Applicant, his Proposer and Seconder, both being in good standing, were this afternoon interviewed. All having given satisfactory answers to the question asked of them, The Applicant was advised of the procedure which would ensue.

The Meeting was Closed with a vote of thank to the Chair

Secretary   8/21   Master

Partick Saint Mary's Lodge,
Enquiry Committee,
Sunday 12th September 2021.

PETITION 29   *An Application for Initiation into Freemasonry having been read on Wednesday 1st September 2021, on behalf of Petition 29 Mr Willikens Costa Dos Santos D.O.B ,17/12/1972, Child Care Assistant , P.O.B. Brazil .*
Residing at 3/2 9 Fordyce Street, Partick, Glasgow G11 5PF.
Proposed by Brother Graeme D. Cameron P.M. .
Seconded by Brother Stanley MacLeod PM., and in keeping with Grand Lodge Law No 168 the Applicant, his Proposer and Seconder, both being in good standing, were this afternoon interviewed. All having given satisfactory answers to the question asked of them, The Applicant was advised of the procedure which would ensue.

PETITION 30   *An Application for Initiation into Freemasonry having been read on Wednesday 1st September 2021, on behalf of Petition 30 Mr Mark Andrew McClymont, D.O.B ,3/2/1981, Technical Operator., P.O.B. Bellshill .*
Residing at 3/2 28 Kenoway Drive ,Glasgow G11 7NY.
Proposed by Brother Alan Cuthill P.M.
Seconded by Brother Stanley MacLeod PM., and in keeping with Grand Lodge Law No 168 the Applicant, his Proposer and Seconder, both being in good standing, were this afternoon interviewed. All having given satisfactory answers to the question asked of them, The Applicant was advised of the procedure which would ensue.

The Meeting was closed with a vote of thanks to the Chair.

Secretary   /21   Master

Partick Saint Mary's Lodge,
Enquiry Committee,
Wednesday 29th September 2021.

Enquiry Committee Meeting,
Masonic Temple,
92 Dumbarton Road,
Partick.
Wednesday 29th September 2021.

OPENING	*A Meeting of the above Committee took place on Wednesday 29th September 2021, at 19.30.*	
PRESENT	*Brother Andrew J. McGroarty,*	*Master,*
	Brother Alan Cuthill	*I.P.M.*
	Brother Cristian Urlea.	*W.S.W.*
	Brother James Gallagher.	*W.J.W.*
	Brother Graham A. Agnew P.M.	*Secretary.*
	Brother Johm McK. Leighton	*Treasurer.*

PM's present Brothers, Graeme D. Cameron, Stanley MacLeod.

APOLOGIES

PETITION 33 An Application for Initiation into Freemasonry having been read on Wednesday 1st September 2021, on behalf of Petition 33 Mr Michael Mitchell Cowley, D.O.B ,12/12/1975, Director, P.O.B. Paisley .
Residing at 11 Fischer Garden, Paisley PA1 2ST.
Proposed by Brother Alan Cuthill P.M. .
Seconded by Brother John McKay Leighton , and in keeping with Grand Lodge Law No 168 the Applicant, his Proposer and Seconder, both being in good standing, were this afternoon interviewed. All having given satisfactory answers to the question asked of them, The Applicant was advised of the procedure which would ensue.

There being no further Business the Meeting was closed with a vote of thanks to the Chair.

Secretary *Graham A Agnew*

9/21

Master.

Partick Saint Mary's Lodge,
Enquiry Committee,
Wednesday 29th September 2021.

Enquiry Committee Meeting,
Masonic Temple,
92 Dumbarton Road,
Partick.
Wednesday 29th September 2021.

OPENING   *A Meeting of the above Committee took place on Wednesday 29th September 2021, at 19.30.*

PRESENT

Brother Andrew J. McGroarty,	*Master.*
Brother Alan Cuthill	*I.P.M.*
Brother Cristian Urlea.	*W.S.W.*
Brother James Gallagher.	*W.J.W.*
Brother Graham A. Agnew P.M.	*Secretary.*
Brother John McK. Leighton.	*Treasurer.*

PM's present Brothers, Graeme D. Cameron, Stanley MacLeod.

PETITION 130 *An Application for Affiliation into Partick Saint Mary's Lodge having been read on Wednesday 1st September 2021.*
Brother Michael John Oates M.M. of Beith St John's Lodge No 157.
Residing at 11 Loudon Crescent, Glasgow G12 9AG.
Brother Secretary to write to the Secretary of Beith St John Lodge No 157 to get Brother Oates Masonic Status.
Proposed by Brother Graeme D. Cameron P.M.
Seconded by Brother Stanley MacLeod PM., and in keeping with Grand Lodge Law No 168 the Applicant, his Proposer and Seconder, both being in good standing, were this afternoon interviewed. All having given satisfactory answers to the question asked of them, The Applicant was advised of the procedure which would ensue.

There being no further business the Meeting was Closed and a vote of thanks to the Chair.

Secretary   *Master*

9/21

www.ingramcontent.com/pod-product-compliance
Lightning Source LLC
Chambersburg PA
CBHW081324260726
48662CB00027B/2341